ALL THE TIME

HAPPINESS

CHARLES MUI

ALL THE TIME HAPPINESS

TABLE OF CONTENTS

DEDICATION

To the inspiring leaders and selfless mentors who have illuminated my path and exemplified the greatness of humanity—this book is for you. Your dedication to guiding others toward growth and fulfillment is a beacon of hope and a testament to the profound impact of personal development.

This book is also a tribute to everyone who has stepped into a leadership role, empowering others to rise and thrive. The personal development industry has gifted me with both passion and purpose, and for that, I am endlessly grateful. To the champions of the human spirit who have distilled the wisdom of the ages and shared it with those eager to grow—you have my deepest gratitude. Your contributions feed the minds and fuel the aspirations of those who dare to dream of a better life.

I was fortunate to be introduced to personal development at the age of 19, a time when the idea of living a fulfilling life and taking control of my destiny captured my imagination. Within the personal development community, I found positivity, care, and a nurturing spirit unlike anything I had ever encountered. My mentors were entrepreneurs who had mastered their time, finances, and connections, and they encouraged me to learn, explore, and discover my true passions.

Their influence steered me toward uncovering the deepest desires of my heart and ignited a lifelong commitment to growth. Over the years, countless mentors, trainers, coaches, leaders, business partners, and fellow entrepreneurs have left an indelible mark on my journey, shaping the person I am today.

This book is dedicated to those extraordinary leaders who have poured their wisdom into others, sparking a ripple effect of transformation and empowerment. The guidance I received over two decades ago set into motion an attitude of continuous growth, and it is with immense gratitude that I now offer this book as a way to pay that wisdom forward.

My hope is that this work inspires others to embrace the power of personal development, find their own path to greatness, and, one day, share their knowledge with the next generation of dreamers.

With heartfelt thanks,

Charles Mui

Section 1:
Cultivating an Empowered Mindset

#1 Harnessing the Power of Thought: Unlocking Success through Empowered Thinking

TONE: Empowering, Reflective, Motivational, Optimistic, Inspiring

We are now in a golden era of mankind. For millennia, humans have strived to achieve the level of prosperity we now enjoy. The difference between those who are happy and healthy, benefiting from humanity's achievements, and those who are sad and unwell, struggling to understand how the mind works, comes down to one idea: we become what we think about most.

> **"The mind moves in the direction of our current dominant thoughts."**
>
> **- Earl Nightingale**

To fully embrace the abundance of the 21st century, you must adopt a belief system that attracts, accepts, and activates a lifestyle that manifests happiness. The mind generates two types of thoughts: empowering and disempowering. When you become aware of your thoughts and begin auditing them, you'll notice patterns that repeat themselves. These patterns are responsible for the results you experience today.

By retraining your thoughts to be empowering, you unlock treasures that were previously unavailable to you. However, it's not enough to merely think empowering thoughts; you must also nurture creativity and continuously improve them. Ask yourself, "How can I make this idea even better? How can I reach the ultimate level?" By actively engaging your creativity, you train your mind to uplift your ideas endlessly. This practice leaves less room for disempowering thoughts.

As you continue on the path of empowerment, you will attract more of what you desire. This process works best when you are intentional about your goals and dreams. Once you switch to empowering thoughts, your aspirations will be continuously nurtured and expanded. Empowered thinking feeds itself, which is what happy, healthy, and successful people do.

It is natural to have fearful, negative, and disempowering thoughts. These thoughts are a normal part of the human experience and have played a role in keeping us safe throughout history. However, an evolved thinker recognizes these patterns and reframes negative ideas into positive ones. Most disempowering thoughts are simply fabrications our brains create; they haven't actually occurred. Since they are merely negative imaginings, we can re-imagine them into uplifting, empowering ideas. This is the power of evolved thinking—the ability to use our God-given gift of creativity to live a happy, magical life.

> **"The seeds of a happy healthy existence are found in empowering ideas. The fertilizer to make it grow is creativity"**
>
> **- CM**

Ask yourself: What disempowering thoughts can I reframe right now?

Action step: Identify an empowering thought that makes you happy and boost it up with some creative thinking to make it the ultra-ultimate.

#2 Creative Living: Designing a Life of Joy and Freedom

TONE: Harmonious, Calming, Introspective, Grounding Inspiring

Eliminate "happiness poverty" through creative living. Creative living is about expressing yourself freely and allowing yourself the joy of designing the lifestyle of your dreams. Humans are naturally built for creative living—we have all the talents and tools embedded in our DNA. We are innately inquisitive, curious, innovative, pleasure-seeking, and adaptive.

When we focus on what brings us joy, we can channel our creativity toward innovative ways of finding happiness. While there are essential responsibilities in life—such as caring for ourselves and our dependents—pleasure-seeking must be balanced with a sustainable way of living. However, creative living is often fueled by struggle, hard work, and increased challenges. The father of invention is the desire to avoid pain, while the mother is the pursuit of pleasure. By harnessing these emotional drivers, we can eradicate happiness and poverty and unlock an endless connection to our divine creative potential.

> **"To live a creative life, one must lose the fear of being wrong"**
>
> **- Joseph Chilton Pearce**

When you adopt a mindset of service to others and free yourself from conditioned thinking, you'll free yourself from depressive thoughts. The first step to "constant happiness" is directing your thoughts toward expanding your freedom. Once you envision your life as a free spirit, your innate creative abilities will generate ideas to manifest that lifestyle. The key is to become aware of new ideas as they emerge in your conscious mind.

Since the moment you were conceived, you've been using your God-given creative abilities. You've created a path to survival and found ways to experience pleasure and happiness. Now, you can use those same abilities to experience happiness more frequently—or even all the time. Happiness is generated through a combination of fun, service, and creation. When you align these three aspects in your life, sadness and depression will fade away.

Creative living is about inventing paths to your joy. Your subconscious is always seeking happiness, but distractions constantly assault it. Media, societal norms, your environment, and countless joy-stealing ideas can derail your pursuit of happiness. You must rise above these distractions and become aware of the external forces that try to influence you. Stay above the noise by connecting to the divine and trusting your instincts to guide you. Your instincts are designed to keep you safe and steer you toward opportunities for joy.

> **"Creativity is the superhighway to happiness"**
>
> **- CM**

The challenge many people face is that they allow fear to dictate their path. When you align yourself with fun and service, all you need to do is become aware of your instinct for joy-seeking—and then take action. Once you take that initial step, the creative process kicks in. You'll naturally begin inventing new ways to bring more joy into your life.

Creative living is about innovating and carving out your own path to happiness. Free yourself from conditioned responses and societal programming. You know what's best for you, and only you can create a path of continuous joy. Even during difficult times, you can still find happiness. When you have the certainty that future happiness awaits you, you'll naturally attract the path to that future. By living as a free spirit, you are empowered to create any path you choose.

> **"A creative life is an amplified life. It's a bigger life, a happier life, an expanded life, and a hell of a lot more interesting life. Living in this manner—continually and stubbornly bringing forth the jewels that are hidden within you—is a fine art, in and of itself."**
>
> **- Elizabeth Gilbert**

Ask yourself: When am I using my creative abilities to generate more happiness?

Action step: Meditate with the intention of connecting to what brings you joy. Then take action on a new idea to manifest that joy in your day.

#3 Aligning with Life's Rhythms:
Harnessing the Power of Seasons for Peak Performance

TONE: Imaginative, Expansive, Playful, Open-Minded

There is a time of day when you are most sharp, alert, and clear. The same applies to your month, year, and life. Humans operate in rhythms, and these cycles help us reach our peak states. Understanding how to harness the natural seasons of life is wisdom in action. Only through experiencing many seasons can you truly understand how you perform during each one. It takes consistency and repetition to attune yourself to the natural flow of your personal cycles. Tuning your life is like tuning an instrument—you must first know when it's in harmony. Dialing in your life requires constant adjustments to get it just right. Most people don't recognize when they are in sync with their optimal performance. The average person is often unaware of when their body, mind, or energy levels are functioning at their best. However, world-class champions operate like finely tuned machines. They know which fuel makes them run best, which time of day they are most alert, and which season they are in.

> "RELAX, everything is running on its own schedule"
>
> - The Universe

Like plants that bloom at different times—whether in winter, summer, spring, or fall—humans also have their seasons. Plants don't consciously choose when to bloom; they are naturally aligned with divine rhythms. Humans, on the other hand, face countless distractions that disconnect us from our natural cycles. Media, technology, and other external influences constantly assault our conscious minds, pulling us away from our innate rhythms.

We are cosmic beings, sharing the same seasons and cycles as the universe. Having the wisdom to synchronize our lives with the natural forces that govern all living things can greatly enhance our well-being. Trying to force outcomes when the timing is off can lead to failure. Relationships, for example, thrive and wither according to seasons. As we mature, our personal seasons will occasionally align with others, and during these times of harmony, it's possible to experience quantum leaps in personal success.

Champions have the wisdom to seize these moments and maximize the potential of that season, manifesting rapid results. Letting go of losing situations, relationships, and patterns is the only way to allow the natural rhythms of life to realign. When everything is clicking, embrace the ride. Surrender to the natural flow and indulge in the winning.

> "Trying to fight the natural rhythms of life is like trying to stop the wind." -CM

> "Everything in the universe has a rhythm, everything dances" - Maya Angelou

> **Ask yourself:** What emotional season am in today, this week, this month, this quarter, this year, this decade?

> **Action step:** Meditate for 30 minutes in silence with the focus on determining what season you are experiencing in your life today.

#4 Embracing Your Unique Gifts:
Building Self-Worth and Letting Go of Comparison

TONE: Focused, Purposeful, Structured, Determined, Resilient, Empowering

The reputation you have with yourself is your self-image. At some point, everyone experiences feelings of inferiority. The truth is we are all inferior or superior to others in different ways. You possess unique skills, attributes, and talents that are entirely your own. The gifts you've been blessed with are amplified by the people you've met, the experiences you've had, and your connection to divine intelligence.

For instance, the most creative mind might not excel in providing support. The best engineer might not be skilled in the art. The boldest leader might lack humility. The question is not whether you're smart but how you are smart.

Comparing yourself to others is a losing game. There will always be someone bigger, faster, or wealthier. What we must realize in order to be happy is that everything changes. What is happening now will not stay the same. The only constant in life is change.

At this moment, your feelings of inferiority may be limiting your happiness. If that's the case, it's entirely because you haven't recognized your unique gifts. By focusing on building credibility with yourself, you can learn to love your talents and share them confidently with the world.

> **"The power of a man's spirit is in direct proportion to a man's loving reputation with himself."**
>
> **- CM**

> **"However difficult life may seem there is always something you can do and succeed at."**
>
> **- Stephen Hawking**

> **Many a superior brain is blocked by inferior thoughts"**
> **-Henry S. Haskins**

> **Ask yourself:** How can I best express my unique gifts to someone I care about in order to make their day better?

> **Action step:** Monitor your thoughts for the next 24 hours and determine if you are comparing yourself to others. If you are comparing, figure out what triggers you to think that way.

#5 The Power of Imagination:
Reframing Life and Unlocking Infinite Possibilities

Imagination is more important than memory. We are all blessed with imperfect memories, and that's a good thing. Forgetting the bad experiences allows us to move forward. Yes, we also forget the good, but this is where imagination becomes more powerful than memory. With imagination, we can envision an infinite number of possibilities for our lives. We can even re-imagine past memories.

The truth is, most of what we remember isn't perfectly accurate. We only recall about 20% of a live presentation, for example. Memory is complex—it's not just words we recall. We subconsciously remember smells, sounds, physical sensations, emotions, and other sensory details. This complexity makes memory unreliable, often distorting events.

> **"The obvious secret most people don't understand is that Imagination is humanity's super power!" - CM**

Imagination, on the other hand, has the power to transport us and shift our mental and physical state in deeply personal ways. We can re-imagine a past event and transform it into something empowering. Imagination allows us to take a negative, traumatic experience and reshape it into something beautiful.

The power of imagination can uplift our spirits, fuel our creativity, and provide relief from depression. When we actively engage our imagination in a positive way, it energizes us and promotes happiness. As human beings, we are gifted with creative thinking, and with that ability, we've shaped the world around us. Our incredible lifestyles are the result of imaginative, creative thought processes.

> **"Imagination is everything. It is the preview of life's coming attractions."**
>
> **- Albert Einstein**

No matter what challenges we face, there is always a creative solution. Believing in the power of imagination is like having a key to unlock any situation. By training your mind to use creativity to rethink and reframe your life, you build momentum toward your goals "Using imagination to set meaningful goals, and then applying creative thinking to generate solutions, is what makes life champions."

> **The world is a canvas for your imagination, you are the painter and there are no rules." - Unknown**

> **Ask yourself:** How can I maximize my incredible gift of imagination right now to improve my happiness?

> **Action step:** Set aside time in a quiet place with a pen and paper. Imagine your perfect day in great detail—from the moment you wake up to the time you go to bed. This exercise will give you a clearer outlook on life and help you identify what truly matters for your happiness

#6 Escape the Prison of Perception: Free Yourself from Limiting Beliefs

Many people find themselves trapped in a prison of perception, feeling little to no hope for their future. The assumptions they make about their ability to shape their own lives limit their imagination and restrict their possibilities. This self-imposed prison is made up of bars, bricks, and guards, all of which are imaginary, yet they feel very real. These mental walls are lies that have been learned and programmed into the subconscious from outside influences—whether from family, society, or personal experiences.

> **"Are you bigger than your bad habits or are your habits bigger than you?"**
>
> **- CM**

At times, these walls may have been put up to protect you. They may have served a powerful purpose at one point in your life, keeping you safe from harm or disappointment. But as life changes, the same walls that once kept you safe can now hold you back from achieving your full potential. Over time, the patterns that were once meant to protect you become habits and routines that run your life on autopilot. While life may continue, you're not truly living if you're confined to predictable patterns that stifle your personal growth.

> **"The only real prison is fear, and the only real freedom is freedom from fear."**
> **– Aung San Suu Kyi**

Routine can be a trap. The comfort of a predictable schedule and habits can become a prison, blocking your access to unlimited potential. It also robs you of the growth opportunities that stem from stepping into the unknown. As humans, we have a deep need for uncertainty, challenges, and new experiences. The human spirit thrives on variety and adventure, and when your life becomes too predictable, your subconscious will create challenges and disruptions to break the monotony.

If you don't proactively seek out challenges and growth, life will force them upon you. It's part of the human condition to need uncertainty for sanity and happiness. When we resist uncertainty out of a desire for comfort, we imprison ourselves in fear of the unknown. This leads to dissatisfaction and, eventually, unhappiness. Personal growth is the source of true happiness, and it's your choice whether to break free from the assumptions and perceptions that limit you or stay confined in a prison of your own making. You have the power to alter your perception and tell yourself new truths that empower you to create the life you truly desire. Escaping the prison of perception requires courage, the willingness to challenge your comfort zone, and a commitment to growth. Don't let fear or routine keep you from the magnificent future that awaits you.

> **Action step:** Pick one comfort in your life that you know is holding you back. It could be food, smoking, a relationship, a job, or any other habit that's imprisoning your ultimate happiness. Commit to breaking that habit by replacing it with a more empowering one. Set yourself free from the chains that bind you.

> **Ask yourself:** What assumption or routine in my life is holding me back from my true potential, and how can I break free from it?

#7 The Power of the Future:
Shaping Your Emotional State and Happiness

TONE: Freeing, Empowering, Enlightening, Transformative, Uplifting, Empowering

Feeling stuck, depressed, or down with life is often a direct symptom of having a poor relationship with your future. 100% of how you feel at any given moment is based on how you perceive your future. Your conscious and subconscious mind is constantly thinking about what's ahead. Human nature is designed in such a way that we create patterns to protect ourselves, and our minds play out these patterns in future scenarios to help us avoid pain. While these patterns can serve us at times, keeping us safe, they are not always conducive to happiness. In fact, they are often the root cause of much of our despair.

"Any thoughts about the future are lies, so you might as well tell ones that leave you empowered."
– CM

To navigate through the thought patterns that serve us and those that no longer do, we can use the power of the future. Whatever is happening in your life today is 100% of your creation. Taking ownership of your life—whether good, bad, or ugly—is the first step in identifying the patterns that are holding you back from joy and happiness. Your mind projects potential future scenarios, recalling attitudes and patterns from your past. However, the past feelings projected into your future are lies—they haven't happened yet. These automatic thoughts, programmed into your subconscious, aim to keep you safe, but they don't always serve your happiness.

"My dreams are my dress rehearsals for my future."

– David Copperfield

When you feel unhappy about your future, your present state reflects that exact unhappy future—but remember, it's a lie because it hasn't happened yet. To change how you feel in the present, you must first change how you see your future. The easiest way to do this is by exercising your imagination and creating your own magnificent future. Envision your ultimate future self: What admirable qualities and attributes does this future version of yourself possess? What kind of lifestyle does this future self-enjoy?

"Your future is a blank canvas, and you are the artist—paint it with bold, empowering visions."

– Unknown

When you emotionally connect to this happy, healthy, positive, thriving version of yourself, a chain reaction of miracles begins to unfold. The universe starts to conspire and attract your magnificent future into your reality. As challenges arise, you will be able to overcome them by consulting with your all-knowing, awesome future self. The stronger the relationship you have with your future self, the easier it becomes to tap into the divine intelligence of the universe for your joy and happiness.

Make your future self your best friend. You can either go through life questioning your existence, making up disempowering lies about being a victim, or you can create your dreams by tuning into the frequencies that attract the lifestyle you desire, how we perceive the future controls our emotional state in the present. Since the future hasn't happened yet, all we're telling ourselves are lies. The choice is yours: Will you tell yourself empowering lies or disempowering ones? You can control your emotional state by envisioning a magnificent future. The more you connect with this ideal future, the more coincidences will occur, drawing that vision into your reality.

Ask yourself: How do I perceive my future, and how can I reframe my vision to empower my present self?

Action step: Take time to write down the qualities and lifestyle of your ultimate future self. How do they live? What habits, values, and traits do they embody? Make a habit of connecting emotionally with this vision every day, and watch as your life begins to align with this powerful future.

#8 Mastering Your Inner Dialogue: Rewriting the Stories You Tell Yourself

TONE: Exciting, Bold, Growth-Oriented, Courageous, Expansive

The most powerful voice in your life is the one inside your own head. Your inner dialogue—the thoughts and beliefs you continuously repeat to yourself—creates your reality. It influences how you perceive the world, how you respond to challenges, and how much happiness and success you believe you deserve. Unfortunately, many of us are running on autopilot, allowing a negative or self-defeating inner narrative to shape our lives. The good news is that you have the power to rewrite those stories and cultivate an empowered mindset that serves your highest potential.

> **"Whatever story you tell yourself about your future is a lie. You can either tell yourself empowering stories or disempowering lies." - CM**

Mastering your inner dialogue begins with awareness. You can't change what you don't recognize, so the first step is to listen to the stories you're telling yourself. Are you constantly criticizing your abilities or doubting your worth? Do you default to fear and insecurity when facing new challenges? The stories you tell yourself may not even be your own. Often, they've been shaped by external influences—society, family, and past experiences. But just because those thoughts have been with you for a long time doesn't mean they're true.

Once you become aware of the limiting beliefs or negative self-talk you've been carrying, it's time to reframe and rewrite those stories. The key to changing your mindset is shifting from disempowering thoughts to empowering ones. For example, instead of saying, "I'm not good enough to achieve this," you can reframe it to, "I have the ability to learn and grow, and I'm worthy of success." It may feel unnatural at first, but with practice, this new dialogue will become your default mode of thinking.

Rewriting your inner narrative isn't about naive optimism or ignoring challenges—it's about shifting your focus to solutions and possibilities rather than obstacles and limitations. When you see yourself as capable, resilient, and worthy, you invite more opportunities for growth and success into your life. Your inner dialogue shapes your outer reality, and by consciously choosing empowering thoughts, you set yourself on a path toward fulfillment and happiness.

It's also important to remember that this process requires consistency. Building an empowered mindset is a lifelong practice. You won't always get it right, and there will be moments when negative thoughts creep back in. But by regularly monitoring and adjusting your inner dialogue, you become better equipped to handle life's challenges with confidence and grace.

"Change your thoughts and you change your world."

– Norman Vincent Peale

Ask yourself: What stories am I telling myself that no longer serve me, and how can I rewrite them to align with my highest potential?

Action step: For the next week, commit to identifying any negative or limiting thoughts you have throughout the day. Write them down and then rewrite them into positive, empowering statements. Notice how this shift in language begins to change your mindset.

#9 Fearless Thinking:
Unlocking Courage and Confidence in Everyday Life

TONE: Patient, Reflective, Peaceful, Grounded, Purposeful Expansive

Fear is one of the most powerful emotions we experience, and it's also one of the most limiting. It keeps us locked in our comfort zones, prevents us from taking risks, and stops us from living our fullest lives. While fear is a natural response designed to protect us, the truth is that most of the fears we experience today are mental barriers rather than actual threats to our survival. Fearless thinking is not about eliminating fear altogether—it's about understanding it, reframing it, and learning to act in spite of it.

"Fear gives birth to doubt and feeds procrastination. Faith promotes action."

- CM

Courage is not the absence of fear. It's the ability to move forward even when fear is present. The key to unlocking courage and confidence in your everyday life begins with your thoughts. Fear often stems from self-doubt, past failures, or the unknown. But these are just stories your mind tells you to keep you "safe." By changing your relationship with fear and approaching it from a place of curiosity rather than avoidance, you can start to break down its power over you.

"Courage doesn't mean you don't get afraid. Courage means you don't let fear stop you."

– Bethany Hamilton

To cultivate fearless thinking, you must first acknowledge your fears. Suppressing or ignoring them only makes them more powerful. Instead, take the time to recognize when fear is showing up in your life. Ask yourself, "What am I really afraid of?" Is it the fear of failure, judgment, or rejection? Once you identify the root cause of your fear, you can begin to dismantle it.

Reframing your fear is one of the most powerful tools in developing fearless thinking. Instead of seeing fear as a roadblock, view it as an opportunity. Fear is often a signal that you are on the verge of growth, stepping into new territory, or challenging your limits. When you reframe fear as a natural part of the journey to success, you can begin to embrace it as a tool for progress rather than something to avoid.

Confidence comes from taking action in the face of fear. The more you confront your fears, the more you realize they aren't as insurmountable as they seem. With each challenge you face head-on, you build courage. This courage doesn't happen overnight, but with consistency, your confidence will grow. You will begin to trust in your own ability to handle whatever comes your way, whether that's a difficult conversation, a new career opportunity, or a personal goal.

Fearless thinking also involves letting go of the need for perfection. Fear often arises when we feel we need to have everything figured out before we take action. But waiting for the perfect conditions or the perfect moment only keeps us stuck. Accept that mistakes and setbacks are part of the process and that courage is built through imperfect action. Each small step forward builds momentum, and with momentum comes greater confidence.

Finally, surround yourself with positive influences. Fear can often be reinforced by the people we surround ourselves with, especially if they project their own doubts and insecurities onto us. Make a conscious effort to seek out people who inspire and support you—people who encourage you to think big, take risks, and believe in your potential. Their energy will help fuel your own fearless thinking.

Ask yourself: Have I been avoiding something due to fear? How can I reframe my fear into an empowering challenge?

Action step: This week, identify one fear that has been holding you back from pursuing something meaningful. Write down the worst-case scenario if you were to face that fear. Then, write down the best-case scenario. Take one small action toward confronting that fear, and notice how your confidence grows with each step.

#10 Breaking the Chains of Comfort: Growth through New Experiences

TONE: Reflective, Thoughtful, Transformative, Enlightening, Insightful

The only difference between who you are today and who you will become tomorrow lies in the people you meet, the books you read, and the experiences you have. Growth happens when you push yourself beyond the boundaries of your comfort zone. Every time you step into the unfamiliar, you expand your horizons and create more capacity for a magnificent life. The more you challenge yourself, the more you realize how limitless your potential truly is.

> **"If you want to be safe, get locked into a jail cell."**
>
> **– CM**

Maturity comes with understanding, and that understanding is earned through a lifetime of experiences. With every challenge, win, and loss, you develop a deeper character and a greater sense of resilience. These experiences allow you to see the world in ways that were previously invisible to you. The most accomplished individuals throughout history share a common trait—they don't avoid obstacles. They choose the obstacle as the path. Instead of seeing challenges as roadblocks, they see them as opportunities for growth, and through this mindset, they forge their own success.

> **"Life begins at the end of your comfort zone."**
>
> **– Neale Donald Walsch**

Comfort is a tempting illusion. While it may feel safe, comfort zones are mental prisons that limit your potential. The more you retreat into comfort, the more you rob yourself of the experiences that could elevate your life to extraordinary levels. Growth requires discomfort, uncertainty, and even failure. It's through these moments of challenge that you gain new insights, discover hidden strengths, and push past the limitations you once thought were unbreakable.

Your dreams are your creative vision for your life in the future. But to make those dreams a reality, you must break free from the familiar. You have to become comfortable with the unknown and the uncertain. Only then can you fully tap into the power of your imagination to envision a future filled with possibility. Stretching your reality through new experiences gives you the power to create a vision of a magnificent future for yourself—a future that wouldn't have been possible had you stayed locked in the safe confines of your comfort zone.

Ask yourself: Am I actively challenging myself, or have I become locked in the mental prison of my own comfort zone?

Action step: Identify one area of your life where you've been playing it safe. Choose an action that pushes you outside of your comfort zone, whether it's meeting new people, trying a new activity, or taking on a new challenge. Reflect on how this experience helps expand your vision of what's possible.

Section 2:
The Power of Action and Momentum

#11 Harnessing Momentum:
The Key to Achieving Your Dreams

TONE: Magical, Serendipitous, Aligned, Purposeful, Expansive

The laws of physics tell us that an object at rest stays at rest. This principle applies not only to the physical world but also to our lives. Nothing in your life will change dramatically until an internal or external force pushes you in a new direction. While change is inevitable, it's entirely up to you whether that change will lead to greater happiness.

"Consciously celebrating wins in your life no matter how small or large will build a pattern of success for you to accomplish anything" - CM

The chance that a change will work in your favor increases dramatically if you are the one who initiates it. This requires motivation, action, and a shift in your thinking to build new momentum. Once momentum is in your favor, it can trigger quantum leaps in the quality of your life. Momentum feeds on itself: just as an object in motion stays in motion, the energy you create will continue to propel you forward unless disrupted by external forces.

Challenges and roadblocks are inevitable on the path to achieving your dreams. However, with enough momentum and belief in yourself, you can power through these obstacles. Momentum helps fuel passion, energy, and enthusiasm, keeping you motivated as you work toward your goals.

"Momentum producers understand an important law of physics: 'objects at rest have momentum.' They know the power of their thinking, planning and acting. Bottom line - - momentum producers are hard to stop."

- David Polly, founder, The Momentum Project

Every time you celebrate a win, no matter how small, you build more velocity toward your vision of the future. As your momentum builds, it will create a powerful energy vortex that acts like a magnet, attracting the solutions and opportunities you need. When your energy aligns with your thoughts, the law of attraction works in your favor, and solutions will begin to appear effortlessly.

The law of attraction has the power to synchronize an infinite number of space and time events to guide you toward a magnificent future filled with all your heart's desires. But it all starts with you initiating positive momentum in your life.

Ask yourself: What can I do right now to inspire more positive momentum toward my dreams?

Action step: Change your body language to create more momentum in your life. For the next 24 hour move, walk, gesture and motion with the attitude to create more momentum in your life.

#12 Creating Momentum:
Harnessing Energy to Propel Your Dreams

TONE: Magical, Serendipitous, Aligned, Purposeful, Empowering Expansive

The greatest catalyst for change is momentum. The beautiful thing about momentum is that it can be created through sheer willpower. While energy cannot be created or destroyed, it can be harnessed and directed. Basic physics tells us that for every action, there is an equal and opposite reaction. This means the amount of energy you put toward your vision will directly determine the progress you experience.

"A problem can not be solved at the same consciousness at which it was created"

- Albert Einstein

However, if your energy is used inefficiently, it will either take longer to reach your goal, or you may burn out before getting there. That's why it's essential to use your energy harmoniously. When you do, growth feels like a magical journey rather than a chore. There are divine patterns in nature and the universe that, when followed, make for a graceful path. Energy can be aligned in ways that attract more energy, causing your progress to grow exponentially.

These patterns, seen throughout human history, are often displayed as sacred geometry. Like attracts like, and when conditions are set up properly, a vortex of energy can be created. This vortex, much like a tornado, harnesses power and sets it into a harmonious pattern, creating massive change. But unlike a tornado, the energy vortex you create doesn't need to be destructive—it can birth some of the most beautiful things in the universe.

An energy vortex disrupts the status quo, accelerating evolution and growth. Flowers, plants, fruits, and even planets use these sacred energy patterns to create life and momentum. You have the power to do the same. With your thoughts, you can create your own vortex of power to influence and bring about change.

Masters of change understand that by manifesting a series of results leading toward an ultimate goal, they empower their ideas into an unstoppable force. To create massive change in your life, align the velocity of your ideas with the frequency of divine harmony. Once you reach that level, the law of momentum will take over, propelling your dreams forward.

At 212 degrees Fahrenheit, water boils and transforms from a liquid into a gas. A magical shift occurs when this boiling point is reached. What is the "boiling point" of your dream?

"When the speed of an organization, individual or idea increases its velocity it will attract more" - CM

Action step: Bring an idea you are passionate about to the point of boiling. Amplify your excitement about an idea over and over again until the idea reaches a boiling point and transforms into something you can be obsessed with.

Ask yourself: What level of energy do I need to generate today to turn my dreams into reality?

#13 Focus, Flow, and Obsession: Unlocking High Performance through Momentum

TONE: Meaningful, Deep, Authentic, Connected, Purposeful

Focus amplifies results, speed, and efficiency. When you direct your focus positively, it sharpens your attention and eliminates distractions, allowing you to concentrate fully on the task at hand. Progress is often derailed by intrusive thoughts and external disruptions. Focus narrows your options and intensifies your efforts toward a specific outcome.

> **"Focus feeds your freedom, distraction traps your potential"**
>
> **- CM**

Complex projects require careful, step-by-step actions to reach the desired result. Without focus, steps can be missed, skipped, or overlooked entirely. Even a single distraction can disrupt your flow and derail an entire project. This is why top performers create environments that encourage focus and minimize distractions. Immersing yourself in a focused environment helps you enter a flow state—a heightened state of performance where you are fully engaged in the present moment.

> **"Your results are the product of either personal focus or personal distractions. The choice is yours."**
>
> **- John Di Lemme**

Flow dramatically amplifies human performance. It occurs when your focus is fully absorbed in an activity. Interestingly, the majority of results often come from a small fraction of the time spent on a project. For an average performer, 10% to 20% of their work time may generate 80% to 90% of the results. These periods of high productivity occur when focus and flow are maximized.

Reaching a flow state can be optimized by setting yourself up for success. Discover the times of day when you function at your highest level and schedule tasks that launch you into flow during those periods. You can also elevate your energy and focus by tuning into frequencies that raise your vibration—through meditation, music, physical activity, nature, and other sensory experiences. These elements can help you sustain focus and flow, accelerating your results.

The longer you remain in a distraction-free flow state, focused on a specific goal, the faster you will produce results. As you consistently enter flow, you build momentum, which makes it easier to return to that state of heightened focus. Momentum also enhances focus by creating obsession—a positive, natural way to stay engaged without forced effort. Obsession allows you to access the flow state more frequently and programs your subconscious mind to work on solutions even when you're not actively focused on them.

While average performers may spend only 10% to 20% of their time in a high-functioning state, obsessed high performers can spend 50% to 80% of their time in flow, achieving exponential results. Becoming a high performer starts with focus, is optimized through flow, and is amplified by obsession. To achieve this, you must eliminate distractions, create an environment for success, and foster an obsessed mindset.

"You can't do BIG things if you are distracted by small things"

- Unknown

Ask yourself: What things, people, apps, devices, and environmental distractions are hurting my ability to focus?

Action step: Remove five things that create distractions. Delete apps, unplug TVs, block certain people, clean up your personal space, etc.

#14 The Power of Action: Overcoming Fear and Building Momentum toward Greatness

TONE: Genuine, Reflective, Empowering, Honest, Transformative

Action is the most powerful trait of a leader. All the positive words, faith, and thoughts mean nothing if they aren't followed by action. Fear often paralyzes action, and it's the number one reason many people never start. However, champions are not necessarily more courageous than the average person—they simply believe that any mistake, setback, or loss can be corrected.

"Leaders are not afraid to fail because the course can always be corrected." - CM

When you operate from a mindset of love, you become more capable of finding solutions and navigating challenges. Love is the frequency of creation and the key to your divine connection with infinite intelligence. With love in your heart, your intentions will be guided by a higher connection, and the actions you take will lead you toward accomplishing your dreams.

"Wisdom and Faith uninvested in labor is wasted"

- Jim Rohn 1930-2009

Action creates momentum, and massive action creates massive momentum. Consistent, persistent, and enthusiastic action generates a gravitational pull toward your goals. As your ideas gain momentum and this gravitational force grows stronger, you'll find yourself plowing through challenges and recovering quickly from setbacks.

No amount of planning can replace the power of action. Planning alone cannot reveal the real-world problems that action will expose and help you overcome. Procrastination is the killer of great ideas, while action is the catalyst for greatness.

Ask yourself: Why do I hesitate when I know the right thing to do?

Action step: Write down task that you have been procrastinating on then imagine the task being completed. Feel the emotion you have knowing the task in over with.

#15 Make Success an Emergency: Harnessing Urgency for Creative Solutions

TONE: Resilient, Strong, Determined, Courageous, Uplifting, Transformative

Make success an emergency. When you approach your goals with the urgency and emotion that an emergency brings, you unlock a level of awareness that can birth new ideas and breakthroughs. Emergencies heighten your senses, forcing you to think quickly, and problem-solve creatively, and push beyond your perceived limits. The key to mastering this state of heightened awareness is to challenge yourself with extreme experiences—situations that stretch you beyond your comfort zone. The more you immerse yourself in these challenging moments, the better you will become at transmuting the stress, adrenaline, and intensity of the experience into fast, creative solutions.

"Procrastination is the killer of great ideas."

- CM

If you continually avoid difficult or high-stress situations, you miss out on the opportunity to build the mental fortitude needed to succeed when it matters most. In emergencies, your body's survival systems kick in, connecting you instantly to the infinite intelligence that lies within your DNA. These built-in systems enable humanity to tap into deep reserves of creativity, intuition, and strength during times of crisis. However, if you are unfamiliar with how these sensations feel—if you haven't trained yourself to recognize and utilize them—you may find yourself overwhelmed, unable to access the powerful gifts that come from this heightened state of being.

"Desire is the catalyst that transforms work into pleasure."

– Bob Proctor

Within every challenge lies an opportunity for growth. It is only when you step outside of your comfort zone that you can fully realize you're potential. Everyone will face struggles in their lifetime, but the difference between those who survive and those who thrive lies in their ability to find growth within the challenge. The ones who consciously seek out and embrace discomfort are the ones who become masters of adversity.

A master is someone who has trained themselves to unconsciously anticipate problems and effortlessly channel challenges into opportunities for success. A master knows that urgency is constant because time is finite. For them, success is not a far-off goal but an emergency that requires immediate action and attention. And yet, they are at peace with this urgency, knowing that it drives them to new heights and deeper growth.

Ask yourself: What challenge in my life can I reframe into an opportunity for growth, and how can I use the urgency of the moment to drive me toward success?

Action step: Identify a current challenge in your life that feels overwhelming. Reframe it as an opportunity for growth. Write down three ways this challenge can help you develop new skills, perspectives, or strengths, and take one immediate action to start facing it head-on.

#16 Turning Intentions Into Reality: The Art of Taking Bold Action

TONE: Energizing, Dynamic, Grounded, Purposeful, Empowering

Intention is a powerful force. It's the starting point of every dream, every goal, and every desire. But without action, even the clearest and most powerful intentions remain nothing more than thoughts in our minds. The real magic happens when you learn to turn your intentions into reality through bold, decisive action. This is where dreams transform into tangible outcomes, and your vision for the future starts to take shape.

> **"Champions win because they choose to be bold"** - CM

Bold action is not just about doing more; it's about doing what matters most with focus, intention, and courage. Many people spend their lives with good intentions, hoping that somehow, someday, their dreams will come true. But intention without action is like a car without fuel—it has the potential to move, but it's not going anywhere until you power it with action. The art of turning intention into reality begins with understanding that action is the bridge between your thoughts and your goals.

> **"You don't have to be great to start, but you have to start to be great."**
>
> **– Zig Ziglar**

The first step in this process is clarity. You must know exactly what you want to achieve and why it's important to you. Without clarity, your actions will be scattered, and your results will be inconsistent. When you have a clear vision, it becomes easier to take action because you know what you're aiming for. Write down your intention in specific, measurable terms. The clearer your intention, the more empowered your actions will be.

Once you have clarity, the next step is commitment. Bold action requires a commitment to follow through, even when it's uncomfortable. It's easy to take action when motivation is high, but the real test comes when you're faced with obstacles, doubt, or fear. Commitment means deciding in advance that you'll keep moving forward, no matter what challenges arise. Bold action is about pushing through resistance—whether that resistance comes from within you or from external circumstances.

Another critical element in turning your intentions into reality is to take the first step immediately. Too often, people spend so much time planning and perfecting their ideas that they never actually begin. Action doesn't have to be perfect; it just has to happen. The sooner you take that first step, the more momentum you build. Bold action thrives on momentum, and once you start moving, it's much easier to keep going. Each small step compounds into larger results over time.

Fear and self-doubt are inevitable when taking bold action, but they don't have to stop you. Courage is built through action, not before it. If you wait until you feel completely confident or prepared, you may never start. Instead, trust that clarity and commitment will guide you, and recognize that every bold action you take builds your confidence. You'll learn as you go, and each step forward will reveal the next one.

Finally, surround yourself with a supportive environment. Bold action requires energy, focus, and resilience, and the people around you can either support or sabotage your efforts. Choose to spend time with those who encourage your growth, who believe in your vision, and who will hold you accountable to your intentions. When you create an environment that fuels your bold actions, success becomes inevitable.

Ask yourself: What intention have I been holding back on, and what bold action can I take today to turn it into reality

Action step: Write down one clear intention you've been holding onto but haven't acted on. Then, commit to taking one bold step toward it within the next 24 hours—whether it's making a phone call, signing up for a class, or setting a meeting. Notice how taking this first step builds momentum.

#17 Disciplined Actions Repeated Over Time: Multiply Your Rewards with Consistency

TONE: Bold, Empowering, Courageous, Action-Oriented

Success isn't the result of a single bold move or an overnight transformation. Success is built through disciplined actions repeated consistently over time. It's the small, deliberate steps taken day after day that lead to massive, long-lasting rewards. Whether you're pursuing personal growth, career goals, or a healthier lifestyle, the key ingredient to achieving those rewards is consistency. It's through repetition, even when progress seems slow that you multiply your results and create the life you desire.

> "The compounding effect of doing the right thing generates exponential results."
> -CM

Discipline and consistency are the foundation of momentum. It's easy to get motivated at the start of a new goal—there's excitement, energy, and the feeling of a fresh start. But what happens after the initial burst of motivation fades? This is where discipline comes into play. Discipline isn't about doing what's easy—it's about doing what's necessary, even when you don't feel like it. It's the ability to stay committed to your goals when the excitement wears off, and life throws distractions your way.

> "We are what we repeatedly do. Excellence, then, is not an act, but a habit."
>
> – Aristotle

Every time you take a small, consistent action toward your goal, you're building momentum. Each action compounds over time, creating a snowball effect that leads to greater results than you might initially expect. Think of it like planting a seed: the daily effort you put into watering, nurturing, and caring for that seed may not show immediate results, but over time, it grows into something far bigger than what you started with. Discipline and consistency are what allow you to reap the rewards of your efforts, even when the progress feels slow or invisible at first.

The power of discipline lies in the fact that it removes the need for constant decision-making. When you establish discipline as a habit, you don't have to wonder whether or not you'll follow through on your goals today—you've already made the decision. Consistency is about creating systems that make it easier for you to stay on track. For example, if your goal is to write a book, set a disciplined routine where you write for an hour every morning, no matter what. Over time, those small sessions add up, and eventually, you'll have a completed manuscript. The same principle applies to any area of life—fitness, career, relationships, or personal development.

Rewards come to those who stay the course. Many people give up right before they're about to achieve their breakthrough. Why? Because they underestimate the power of discipline and consistency. They grow impatient when results don't happen quickly. But the reality is that most successes are born from persistence. The greatest rewards are often waiting just beyond the point where most people quit. By staying disciplined and committed, even when it's tough, you'll be able to multiply your rewards in ways that others can't.

Another benefit of disciplined, consistent action is that it builds self-confidence and trust in yourself. Every time you follow through on a commitment, you reinforce the belief that you are capable of achieving your goals. You create a positive cycle where consistency leads to progress, progress leads to confidence, and confidence leads to even greater consistency. It's a loop that accelerates your growth and momentum.

Ask yourself: What habit can I create that will ensure a consistent action that will move me towards the lifestyle I want to have?

Action step: Choose one small, disciplined action you can take every day for the next month that moves you toward one of your key goals. Set up a system or routine that makes it easy for you to follow through. At the end of the month, reflect on the progress you've made and how consistency has multiplied your results.

#18 From Stagnation to Flow: Finding Your Rhythm to Stay in Motion

TONE: Consistent, Empowering, Rewarding, Progressive

We've all experienced moments where progress feels impossible. It's as if we're stuck in place, spinning our wheels but not moving forward. This feeling of stagnation can be frustrating and demoralizing, leading us to doubt our abilities and question our path. But stagnation is not permanent. It's simply a temporary pause that can be overcome by finding your rhythm and reconnecting with a state of flow. The key to breaking free from stagnation is to tap into that powerful rhythm, where your actions feel effortless, and progress becomes natural.

> **"Small Steps lead to big leaps"**
>
> **- CM**

Flow is a state of optimal performance where time seems to disappear, and you become fully immersed in the task at hand. When you're in flow, everything feels aligned, and your productivity skyrockets. However, finding flow when you're stuck in stagnation requires a shift in both mindset and attitude. The first step is to acknowledge that stagnation is normal. It's not a sign of failure but rather a signal that something needs to change—whether that's your environment, your habits, or your perspective.

> **"Momentum breeds momentum, and the best way to start is to start."**
>
> **– Gil Penchina**

One of the most effective ways to move from stagnation to flow is by taking small, deliberate actions. Stagnation often occurs when we feel overwhelmed by the size of the task in front of us. We freeze because the goal seems too big or the path too uncertain. But the antidote to this paralysis is simple: start small. Instead of focusing on the entire mountain you need to climb, shift your focus to the next step right in front of you. Take action, no matter how small, and let that first step create momentum.

Momentum is the bridge between stagnation and flow. Once you begin taking action, you'll notice that each step forward makes the next step easier. This is the power of momentum—it compounds with each action, building on itself until you find yourself in a state of flow. Even the smallest action, taken consistently, can create enough momentum to break through the walls of stagnation.

Another crucial factor in finding flow is understanding your personal rhythm. Everyone has a natural rhythm for productivity and creativity. For some, it's early in the morning; for others, it's late at night. Pay attention to when you feel most energized and focused throughout the day. Once you identify your rhythm, align your most important tasks with those peak times. Working with your natural energy flow rather than against it will help you stay in motion and achieve a state of flow more consistently.

In addition to small actions and personal rhythm, it's important to create an environment that supports flow. Stagnation can often be the result of a cluttered or distracting environment. Whether it's your physical space or your mental space, distractions drain your focus and make it harder to stay in motion. Clear out unnecessary clutter, eliminate distractions, and create a space that inspires creativity and focus. When your environment is aligned with your goals, you'll find it easier to stay in the flow.

Finally, to maintain flow over the long term, take care of your mind and body. Physical well-being plays a significant role in your ability to stay in motion. Regular exercise, sufficient rest, and proper nutrition all contribute to a sharper mind and more consistent energy levels. When your body is taken care of, your mind can focus more easily, allowing you to slip into flow with less effort.

Ask yourself: Where in my life am I experiencing stagnation and how much has it costed me by not taking action?

Action step: Identify one area of your life where you feel stuck or stagnant. Break down your goal into small, manageable tasks and commit to taking one action today, no matter how small. Track your progress over the next week and notice how even small actions create momentum and shift you toward flow.

#19 Momentum Mastery:
How to Keep Moving Forward No Matter What

TONE: Trustworthy, Honest, Grounded, Empowering

Momentum is one of the most powerful forces in your life. When you're in motion, everything seems easier—opportunities flow to you, tasks get done faster, and progress feels inevitable. But momentum isn't just about those times when everything is going well. True momentum mastery is the ability to keep moving forward, no matter what obstacles or setbacks come your way. It's the skill of maintaining motion when life throws challenges, distractions, or doubts at you.

Momentum thrives on consistency. The key to momentum is not grand gestures or rare moments of inspiration. It's about showing up consistently, day after day, even when things aren't going perfectly. Momentum builds when you take action, no matter how small, and stick to your commitments. Each small step forward fuels the next, creating a cycle of forward movement that becomes easier to maintain over time. The beauty of momentum is that it compounds—the more you do, the more energy you have to keep doing.

The biggest threat to momentum is stopping altogether. Once you stop moving, it's incredibly difficult to get started again. Think of a heavy train—once it's in motion, it moves with great force, but it takes tremendous energy to get it started from a standstill. The same is true with your goals and progress. It's easier to keep going than to stop and start again. Even when life gets hard, it's better to take small steps forward than to stop completely when you keep moving, even if at a slower pace, you preserve the momentum you've built.

One of the most effective ways to master momentum is to break big tasks into smaller, manageable actions. When a task feels overwhelming, it's easy to procrastinate or feel paralyzed by the size of the goal. But by breaking it down into bite-sized steps, you not only make progress more achievable, but you also create little victories along the way. Each time you complete a small task, you're reinforcing the habit of moving forward and building confidence in your ability to tackle the bigger challenge.

Momentum mastery also requires mental resilience. Life will throw you curveballs—whether they come in the form of unexpected setbacks, fear, or external distractions. The secret to maintaining momentum through these challenges is to develop the mindset that no matter what happens, you will find a way to keep moving forward. When things go wrong, don't let them derail your progress. Adapt, adjust, and continue. If a plan fails, rework it. If you face rejection, keep trying. Momentum isn't about avoiding failure—it's about using failure as fuel to push forward.

One of the most overlooked elements of maintaining momentum is celebrating your progress. Many people don't take the time to acknowledge the small wins along the way, but these victories are essential for staying motivated and energized. Celebrating progress fuels momentum because it reminds you that you're moving in the right direction, even if the ultimate goal is still far away. By recognizing the progress

> **"Prioritize daily forward progress until the momentum carries itself"**
>
> **- CM**

you've made, you reinforce your belief in your ability to succeed, which makes it easier to keep moving forward.

Finally, surround yourself with positive influences. Your environment plays a significant role in whether you maintain momentum or fall off track. If you're constantly around negativity, doubt, or distractions, it will be harder to stay focused. Conversely, when you're surrounded by people who support your goals, encourage your progress, and celebrate your wins with you, it becomes much easier to keep moving forward. Your environment is either fueling your momentum or depleting it—choose wisely.

> **"Success is the sum of small efforts, repeated day in and day out."**
>
> **– Robert Collier**

Ask yourself: Is there a person or challenge that continues to derail my momentum?

Action step: Identify something or someone that stifles your progress. Evaluate how and why you allow yourself to compromise your momentum. Make a decision to remove this person of thing from your routine for 30 days. After 30 days re-evaluate your decision and determine if the problem was with you or the outside influence.

**#20 Triggering a Flow State:
Complete Engagement in the Present**

TONE: Disciplined, Grounded, Peaceful, Empowering, Purposeful

When you are in a flow state, you are 100% engaged in the present activity. Everything outside the moment fades away, and your entire focus is directed toward the task at hand. Extreme athletes often experience flow when their lives are on the line—whether it's jumping out of an airplane, snowboarding through dense trees, or kayaking down roaring whitewater rapids. These activities thrust them into flow because when your life depends on it, there's no room for distractions. You can't afford to think about the past or worry about the future. You are locked into the present, fully tapping into your instincts, divine intelligence, and spontaneous right action.

> **"Elevate your engagement until all distractions fade away and you arrive at flow"**
>
> **- CM**

> **"The best moments in our lives are not the passive, receptive, relaxing times... The best moments usually occur if a person's body or mind is stretched to its limits in a voluntary effort to accomplish something difficult and worthwhile."
> – Mihaly Csikszentmihalyi**

In these moments, there is no time to dwell on the past, no space to fear what's coming next. Your senses are heightened, and you're completely immersed in the now. The thrill and intensity of the experience naturally propel you into a state of flow, where your performance reaches new heights, and everything feels effortless.

But here's the good news: you don't have to risk your life to enter a flow state. Flow isn't exclusive to extreme athletes or high-stakes situations. You can trigger flow in everyday life by amplifying your rate of vibration and locking into the present moment. It may take some time to warm up, but once you enter flow, you'll notice how seamlessly your mind, body, and spirit align with the task at hand.

One way to enter flow is through activities that naturally demand your full attention. Team sports are a great example, as they introduce an element of accountability. Your teammates rely on you, and this shared responsibility creates a heightened sense of focus and engagement. In team sports, you don't have the luxury of being distracted or stuck in your head; you are pulled into the moment and forced to react instinctively.

Other methods to trigger flow include creating structured routines or rituals that help you tune out distractions and fully immerse yourself in the task. Artists, musicians, and writers often talk about the "warm-up" phase, where they work their way into flow by engaging with their craft repeatedly until they hit that sweet spot of total focus. Finding what pulls you into the present moment, whether it's creative work, exercise, or a mental challenge, will pay huge dividends in your productivity, peace of mind, and overall happiness.

The rewards of flow are immense. When you emerge from a flow state, your body is flooded with adrenaline, endorphins, and dopamine—the chemicals that make you feel incredible. These natural highs leave you feeling energized, clear-headed, and ready for more. It's no wonder that flow creates momentum—it gives you a sense of being unstoppable, a feeling that you can conquer anything that comes your way.

That feeling of unstoppability is where the magic happens. When you're in flow, the impossible begins to feel possible. Even if the odds are stacked against you, or the probability of success is less than 1%, the flow has the power to shift momentum like a tidal wave. In flow, you're not limited by logic or statistics. You're tapped into a higher level of intelligence—one where an unlimited number of space and time events can conspire to bring your desired outcome into a miraculous manifestation.

Flow taps into divine intelligence, and that's why it feels so powerful. It connects you to something beyond yourself, where creativity, intuition, and energy all flow together effortlessly. When you're in flow, you're in harmony with the universe, and in that state, incredible things become possible. You no longer question your capabilities or the path ahead—you just act, create, and achieve.

Ask yourself: What activity or environment pulls me completely into the present moment, and how can I structure my life to experience flow more often?

Action step: Identify an activity in your life where you've experienced glimpses of flow, whether it's a physical challenge, creative work, or problem-solving. Commit to practicing this activity consistently and create a routine that encourages you to enter flow more frequently. Notice how your productivity and mood shift after spending time in flow.

Section 3:

Living with Love and Gratitude:

 # 21 The True Meaning of Respect: Building Healthier Relationships

TONE: Warm, Hopeful, Generous, Compassionate, Altruistic

Always treat others with respect. When reflecting on their lives, people often regret treating others poorly. Nearly all suffering in personal relationships stems from a lack of respect—whether it's respect that was not given or not received. Yet, few people have a clear understanding of what respecting others truly means.

To give respect is not to harm, but to allow others the freedom to express themselves, and to honor the reality that their thoughts, feelings, and actions are valid in their own minds, even if we find them unimportant or disagree with them. Respect doesn't necessarily imply approval. We can respect someone's right to speak without agreeing with what they say.

Respect involves recognizing that others are doing the best they can with what they have, who they are, and the circumstances they've been given, even if we don't see their efforts as admirable. It's about acknowledging the divinity in others and never inviting disrespect into our lives by projecting it onto others.

"Display honor by unconditionally respecting others, even if you do not see eye to eye because your character is best built on principles not judgment" - CM

"Respect yourself enough to walk away from anything that no longer serves you, grows you, or makes you happy" - Unknown

"To get respect you must first give respect"

- Jesse Cieluch

Ask yourself: How can I cultivate more respect within myself for others?

Action step: Follow up with someone that you may have disrespected and give them a sincere compliment about something that you respect them for.

#22 The Power of Gratitude: Transforming Your Life through Appreciation

TONE: Intense, Productive, Focused, Driven, Immersive

Gratitude transforms your mind, body, and spirit like nothing else can. It is the master emotion and the cornerstone of great people's attitudes. When you are in a state of gratitude, you are free from worry, doubt, fear, and other negative emotions. Gratitude cleanses your soul of toxic thoughts and empowers your happiness. There is an infinite number of things to be grateful for, and the more you acknowledge them, the more you will find to be grateful for.

Unlike many other practices, gratitude doesn't require moderation. Most things in life need balance, as excess can lead to burnout or carelessness. But gratitude is different—it thrives the more you practice it. For most people, gratitude starts as a conscious effort, but the truly grateful makes it a permanent mindset. A positive person isn't someone who avoids negativity altogether—that's impossible. Rather, a positive person uses gratitude to transform any situation into something to be thankful for.

When you commit to an attitude of gratitude, you'll begin to repel negativity in all its forms—people, places, and things. At the same time, you'll attract more of what brings you happiness and fulfillment. Gratitude is most powerful when expressed boldly, publicly, with a smile on your face and kindness in your heart. By openly showing gratitude, you make it contagious, and it will inevitably return to you in some form.

> "You possess the magical powers of gratitude. With your gratitude magic you can turn what you have into enough and turn enough into happiness." - CM

> "Gratitude is the healthiest of all human emotions. The more you express gratitude for what you have the more likely you will have even more to express gratitude for."
>
> - Zig Zielger

You cannot overdo gratitude. The more intensely you express it, the brighter the world around you will become—the colors will be more vivid, the sounds sharper, and the love deeper. Gratitude is the master emotion because it shapes your attitude, beliefs, actions, and behaviors. By making gratitude your top priority, you are ensuring yourself a happy, joyful, and blessed life.

Ask yourself: Why haven't I been more extreme with my gratitude? Is there truly any reason not to be grateful?

Action step: Verbally express gratitude to 10 people—boldly and as soon as possible.

#23 The Power of Unconditional Love: Breaking Patterns of Fear

TONE: Persistent, Dynamic, Driven, Resilient

It takes far more nobility, character, and strength to resolve the issues within a trusted relationship than to merely service the superficial needs of the masses. Relationships that truly matter require a deeper level of commitment, patience, and resilience. Unconditional acceptance, understanding, and love are not easily won, but when fought for and manifested, they become a cause for celebration. This kind of love requires effort, a willingness to face difficult conversations, and the strength to confront deep-seated fears. However, the rewards are profound and life-changing.

In many cases, it's the fear of not being fully accepted that creates tension and strain in relationships. When a loved one comes to the realization that they are truly and unconditionally accepted, it's a moment of profound relief. It's not an everyday occurrence to have our spirit tested by such a challenge, but when it happens, and when love is proven to be stronger than fear, a deep transformation takes place. The discovery of a deeper level of love—a love that transcends conditions and expectations—can break patterns of fear that may have existed for years.

> "When fear attacks do not crack just love it back"
>
> – CM

> "Darkness cannot drive out darkness; only light can do that. Hate cannot drive out hate; only love can do that."
>
> – Martin Luther King Jr.

Eliminating fear through the revelation of love emboldens your spirit and raises the quality of your life to a higher level. When we operate from a place of love instead of fear, we experience life more fully, with more joy, confidence, and compassion. By shining the light of love into the darkness of fear, we release more light into the world. This ripple effect can be felt not only within the relationship but also in the larger community, as love has the power to transform both individuals and their environment.

However, the journey toward unconditional love and acceptance is not easy. It requires us to look beyond the surface and truly understand another person's fears and insecurities. To do this, we must practice empathy, patience, and vulnerability. When we take the time to understand someone's fear and love them more for it, we build a foundation of trust that strengthens the relationship. This trust becomes the bedrock upon which deeper connections are formed.

Ask yourself: When was the last time you took the time to understand another's fear and loved them more for it?

Action step: Take some time to reflect on a close relationship in your life. Identify any fears or insecurities your loved one may have expressed. Next, schedule a quiet moment with them, and instead of offering solutions, simply listen and offer unconditional acceptance. Tell them you love them as they are and that their fears do not diminish their worth in your eyes. Observe how this changes the dynamic of the relationship and strengthens your bond.

#24 The Antidote to Entitlement:
Gratitude and the Path to Fulfillment

TONE: Energizing, Revitalizing, Fluid, Motivational

Entitlement is one of the most toxic attitudes a person can have. It weakens the mind, hollows out a person's character, and makes the journey to freedom and fulfillment impossible. At its core, entitlement is the belief that we are owed something, that we deserve more simply because we exist. This mindset blocks personal growth and poisons relationships, as it is rooted in selfishness and lack. When people feel entitled, they become disconnected from the reality that nothing of true value comes without effort, appreciation, and gratitude.

> **"Gratitude is not only the greatest virtue but the path to all others."**
>
> **– Cicero**

Entitlement often leads to plunder—the dishonest and sometimes violent acquisition of things that do not rightfully belong to us. Plunder doesn't have to be physical theft; it can also be the emotional or mental demand for recognition, wealth, or happiness without having earned it. Entitlement clouds our judgment and leads us to believe that we should have more while contributing less. When this mindset takes over, the road to prosperity and abundance becomes impassable. The walls built by entitlement are too high to climb, keeping us stuck in a mindset of scarcity and discontent.

> **"Feeling gratitude and not expressing it is like wrapping a present and not giving it."**
>
> **– William Arthur Ward**

However, the cure for entitlement is gratitude. When we practice gratitude, we shift our focus away from what we think we deserve and toward what we already have. Gratitude opens the door to abundance by changing our energy and mindset. Instead of feeling deprived or envious, we feel blessed. When we express genuine appreciation for the good things in our lives, we connect to a deeper sense of love, joy, and fulfillment. Gratitude empowers us to transform what we have into enough, and in doing so, it creates the right energy to attract even more goodness into our lives.

A life rooted in gratitude is one that is rich in love, connection, and contentment. When we actively show and express our thankfulness, we strengthen our relationships and enhance our own sense of well-being. Gratitude doesn't just benefit us; it ripples out to those around us, creating a more positive and supportive environment. The more thankful we are for what we have been blessed with, the more love we can create in our lives.

Gratitude is a powerful force, one that can turn the smallest things into sources of great joy. When we learn to focus on what we have rather than what we lack, we open ourselves up to receiving even more. It is through gratitude that we break the chains of entitlement and free ourselves to live a life of abundance.

Ask yourself: Where in my life am I feeling entitled, and how can I replace that feeling with gratitude?

Action step: Take five minutes each day to write down three things you are grateful for. Focus on what you already have, rather than what you want. Reflect on how each thing brings value to your life and makes you feel blessed. Share your gratitude with someone by expressing thanks to them directly.

#25 The Power of Love, Happiness, and Gratitude: Manifesting Your Dreams

TONE: Compassionate, Selfless, Connected, Supportive, Empathetic

Happiness and love are two of the most powerful tools you have for creating the lifestyle of your dreams. These emotions vibrate at a high frequency, acting as a catalyst for manifesting your heart's desires into your reality. When you feel happiness and love, you align yourself with the positive energy of the universe, which accelerates the process of turning your dreams into tangible outcomes.

To generate more happiness and love in your life, you must first cultivate gratitude for what you already have. Gratitude is the foundation upon which happiness and love are built. It shifts your focus from what you lack to the abundance that already exists in your life. The simple act of becoming aware of the blessings around you instantly raises your vibration and puts you in harmony with the energy needed to manifest your dreams.

Gratitude is not just a feeling; it's a way of living. It's about becoming aware that every moment you experience is a gift. The present moment is the most valuable thing you have because it's all you're ever truly guaranteed. The present is the key to unlocking your unlimited potential, for it is only in the present moment that you can take action, dream, and create.

When you embrace the present, you open yourself up to limitless possibilities. Your future is only limited by your imagination and your ability to focus your attention. This realization is powerful: you have been granted the divine gift of the present moment, and within it lies the magic to create whatever your heart truly desires. The question then becomes, how will you use this gift?

> **"Gratitude is the foundation to launch your personal rocket of success to unimaginable heights"**
>
> **- CM**

> **"Gratitude opens your eyes to the limitless potential of the universe, while dissatisfaction closes your eyes to it."**
>
> **– Stephen Richards**

> **"Struggle ends when gratitude begins."**
>
> **– Neale Donald Walsch**

Many people spend their time focused on future goals or past regrets, missing out on the beauty and power of now. But the truth is that everything you need to create the life of your dreams is already within you, and it's accessible right now. By living in a state of gratitude, you become more aware of this truth and tap into the infinite potential that exists within the present moment.

"Gratitude is the spark that will ignite your soul on fire with happiness" -CM

Ask yourself: What am I going to do with the gift of "right now" and my magic power to create the life I desire?

Action step: Take a few minutes each morning to reflect on the present moment. Sit quietly, close your eyes, and express gratitude for what you have right now—your health, relationships, opportunities, and the simple gift of being alive. Then, ask yourself what you can do today to make the most of this moment and move closer to your dreams.

#26 The Power of Heart-Centered Generosity: A Universal Balance

TONE: Reflective, Growth-Oriented, Enlightening, Empowering, Purposeful

Generosity, when generated from heart-centered, love-inspired thought, always creates a positive return. When you give to others from a place of love, whether it's your time, resources, or support, you are making deposits into their lives that build not only their spirit but your own as well. These acts of kindness and generosity create a positive balance in your life, one that will inevitably return to you in ways you may not expect. The universe operates with perfect balance and harmony, ensuring that whatever energy we give out will find its way back to us.

> "Generosity is giving more than you think you can and gratitude is taking less than you need" - CM

The concept of karma—the idea that our actions create corresponding reactions in the universe—plays a vital role in how generosity shapes our lives. When you give freely, without expectation of reward, you build a positive balance of karma. You may not always see immediate returns, but rest assured that the universe has its own perfect timing and balancing system. The givers and the takers will always get exactly what they deserve, even if it's not immediately obvious. The beauty of this cosmic balance is that it doesn't require us to monitor or control the outcomes. The infinite intelligence of the universe ensures that everything is kept in perfect equilibrium.

> "No one has ever become poor by giving." – Anne Frank

> "Real generosity toward the future lies in giving all to the present."
>
> – Albert Camus

Generosity isn't just about material giving. It's about sharing love, compassion, understanding, and support with those around you. Sometimes, the most valuable thing you can give someone is your time or a listening ear. These are the gifts that can't be measured in material terms but have a profound impact on both the giver and the receiver. When you give from the heart, you elevate not only the lives of others but also your own soul.

One of the most powerful aspects of generosity is that it fosters connection and trust. When you consistently give to others, you create meaningful relationships that are built on mutual respect and appreciation. This leads to a cycle of giving and receiving that nurtures both the individual and the collective spirit of the community. The more you give, the more you receive—not because you're expecting it, but because the universe naturally aligns to support those who give from the heart.

Ask yourself: In what ways can I give more freely without expecting anything in return, trusting that the universe will maintain the perfect balance?

Action step: Identify one person in your life who could benefit from an act of generosity today. It doesn't have to be material—consider offering your time, support, or a simple gesture of kindness. Reflect on how this act made you feel and the positive energy it brought into both your life and theirs.

#27
Paradigm Shifting: Cultivating an Attitude of Gratitude

TONE: Selfless, Generous, Compassionate, Purposeful, Fulfilling

The modern world has created a confusing narrative around happiness. History has turned happiness into something elusive, a state that supposedly requires struggle, sacrifice, and the attainment of external rewards to achieve. In our society, happiness is often presented as a product—sold to us in the form of a pill, a TV episode, or a drink. We've been conditioned to believe that happiness is something we must chase or buy, something that will only come when we've achieved success, wealth, or some distant goal.

> **"Whether you choose happiness or not you are 100% right, Its just funner to be happy"**
> **- CM**

The truth is happiness is subjective and deeply personal. It means something different to each of us, and it doesn't need to be tied to external circumstances or accomplishments. For many, the idea of experiencing a constant state of happiness is unrealistic or even impossible, a concept scoffed at by thought leaders and psychologists alike. However, the fact remains that happiness can be reached at any moment, no matter the situation. It's a choice—and one that often requires a paradigm shift in how we view our circumstances.

One of the most powerful ways to make this shift is by cultivating an attitude of gratitude. Gratitude has the power to transform how we experience the world. It allows us to reframe challenges, setbacks, and disappointments into opportunities for growth and learning. It moves the goal line of happiness to something much more attainable—the recognition of what we already have and the ability to find joy in the present moment. By shifting our focus from what we lack to what we are grateful for, we can instantly create a mental and emotional shift toward happiness.

This doesn't mean you should be delusional or out of touch with reality. It doesn't mean ignoring pain, challenges, or hardship. Rather, it's about developing the critical thinking and emotional resilience to reframe difficult situations in a way that empowers you rather than bringing you down. When faced with difficulty, you always have a choice: you can either react to the situation with frustration and fear, or you can choose to respond with gratitude and perspective.

Reframing is a powerful tool for shifting your paradigm. When something disrupts your happiness—whether it's a personal challenge, a setback at work, or a difficult relationship—you can choose to see it as an opportunity for growth rather than an obstacle. You might need to sift through some negative thoughts first, and that's okay. It's normal to feel fear or frustration in the face of hardship. However, once you acknowledge those emotions, you have the power to shift your perspective.

Start by asking yourself, "What can I learn from this?" or "How can this experience make me stronger?" These questions help to reframe the situation in a way that empowers you to take control. Instead of being a victim of your circumstances, you become an active participant in your own happiness. This process allows you to find gratitude in even the most challenging situations. You may not be grateful for the hardship

> **"Happiness is not by chance, but by choice."**
>
> **– Jim Rohn**

itself, but you can be grateful for the lessons it teaches, the strength it builds, and the resilience it fosters.

Gratitude shifts your focus from what's wrong to what's right. It reminds you that, despite the challenges you face, there are still things in your life to be thankful for. This could be something as simple as the support of a loved one, the beauty of nature, or the opportunities you have for growth. When you cultivate an attitude of gratitude, you take control of your happiness by choosing to focus on the positive aspects of your life rather than getting lost in the negative.

This kind of paradigm shift requires consistent practice. It's easy to let negative thoughts take over, especially when life gets tough. But with practice, you can train your mind to shift toward gratitude more naturally. By regularly acknowledging the good in your life—no matter how small—you build the mental resilience to handle challenges with grace and positivity.

The beauty of gratitude is that it doesn't depend on your external circumstances. You don't need to be wealthy, successful, or free from problems to feel grateful. Gratitude is available to you at all times, and it's one of the quickest ways to tap into happiness, even in difficult moments. It's a mindset that allows you to rise above your challenges, find joy in the present, and create happiness from within.

Ask yourself: How can I reframe my current challenges in a way that empowers me to find gratitude and happiness in the present moment?

Action step: Start a daily gratitude practice. Each morning, write down three things you are grateful for, no matter how small. As you face challenges throughout the day, pause and ask yourself, "What can I learn from this, and how can I reframe it to empower myself?" Over time, this practice will help you shift your mindset toward gratitude and create lasting happiness.

#28 The Gratitude Effect:
How Thankfulness Unlocks Unlimited Joy

TONE: Liberating, Empowering, Bold, Courageous, Uplifting

Gratitude is one of the simplest yet most powerful practices you can cultivate in life. It's a mindset that shifts your focus from what you lack to what you already have. When you live with a grateful heart, you begin to notice the abundance that surrounds you—things that once went unnoticed now fill you with appreciation. The gratitude effect is real: the more you focus on what you're thankful for, the more joy and fulfillment you attract into your life. Gratitude not only changes how you feel, but it also transforms how you experience the world around you.

> "Gratitude turns what we have into enough."
>
> – Aesop

In today's fast-paced world, it's easy to get caught up in the pursuit of more. We constantly strive for the next achievement, the next purchase, or the next big success, thinking that happiness will come once we reach those milestones. But true joy doesn't come from the endless chase for more. It comes from appreciating what you already have. When you practice gratitude, you create a mental shift that allows you to feel contentment in the present moment, no matter what your circumstances are.

Gratitude has the unique ability to unlock joy, even in difficult situations. It doesn't mean ignoring challenges or pretending everything is perfect—it means finding the silver linings, even in the midst of adversity. When you're able to focus on what's going right rather than what's going wrong, you tap into a powerful source of resilience. Gratitude changes your perspective, and in doing so, it changes how you respond to life's ups and downs. Thankfulness doesn't eliminate hardship, but it gives you the emotional tools to navigate it with grace.

Gratitude is also the key to abundance. When you are grateful for what you have, you signal to the universe that you're open to receiving more. It's a fundamental principle: what you focus on expands. By acknowledging and appreciating the good in your life, you create a positive feedback loop that draws even more goodness toward you. Gratitude becomes a magnet for joy. It amplifies the things you appreciate, and suddenly, you begin to notice even more reasons to be thankful.

Another aspect of the gratitude effect is that it fosters stronger relationships. Expressing gratitude toward others deepens connections and strengthens bonds. When you take the time to thank the people in your life—whether it's for a kind gesture, their support, or simply their presence—you create a sense of warmth and appreciation that enhances the relationship. Gratitude reminds us of our interconnectedness, and when we share it, we spread joy not only to ourselves but to those around us.

> "Appreciation for the small opens up our heart to enjoy all the gratitude for the grandest."
>
> -CM

Gratitude also improves your physical and mental health. Studies have shown that people who practice gratitude regularly experience lower levels of stress, anxiety, and depression. Gratitude has been linked to better sleep, stronger immune systems, and an overall increase in well-being. When you're thankful, your body and mind operate from a place of peace rather than stress. The act of focusing on the positive literally rewires your brain to be more optimistic, creating a cycle of positive emotions and improved health.

The beauty of gratitude is that it's always available to you. No matter where you are in life, no matter what you're going through, there's always something to be grateful for. Whether it's as small as a warm cup of coffee in the morning or as big as the love of your family, every moment holds a potential gift. The more you practice noticing and appreciating these moments, the more joyful your life will become.

Ask yourself: What am I taking for granted? What is something in my life that is an extreme blessing that I do not regularly feel grateful for?

Action step: Start a gratitude journal and commit to writing down three things you're thankful for each day. These don't have to be grand gestures. They can be simple things like opening your eyes, a kind word, or air conditioning. At the end of the week, reflect on how this practice has affected your mood, outlook, and sense of well-being.

**#29 Heart-Centered Leadership:
Leading with Love and Creating Deeper Connections**

TONE: Connected, Joyful, Warm, Supportive, Empowering

True leadership isn't just about authority or power—it's about influence, empathy, and the ability to connect with others on a deeper level. Heart-centered leadership is the practice of leading from a place of love, compassion, and integrity. It's a leadership style that prioritizes relationships, emotional intelligence, and the well-being of others rather than focusing solely on results or personal gain. When you lead from the heart, you not only inspire those around you, but you also create environments where people feel valued, understood, and empowered.

> "To handle yourself, use your head; to handle others, use your heart."
>
> – Eleanor Roosevelt

At the core of heart-centered leadership is the understanding that people are the most important asset. A leader who leads with love knows that relationships, trust, and connection are the foundation of any successful venture, whether it's in business, personal life, or community. When you show genuine care and concern for the people you lead, you create a culture of trust. Trust fosters loyalty, creativity, and innovation, which ultimately leads to greater success.

> "Be the heart centered leader others are looking for and you will inspire others to rise into leadership roles"
>
> - CM

Leading with love means leading with empathy. It's about putting yourself in the shoes of others and understanding their perspectives, challenges, and needs. A heart-centered leader listens actively and with an open mind, making others feel heard and respected. Empathy is a powerful tool that deepens your connection with others because it shows that you care about them not just as employees, colleagues, or followers but as human beings. This type of leadership builds a bond that goes beyond the surface level, creating a strong foundation of mutual respect.

In heart-centered leadership, vulnerability is a strength, not a weakness. Leaders who lead with love are not afraid to show their authentic selves, including their challenges and imperfections. This openness encourages others to do the same, creating an environment of transparency and honesty. When people feel safe to be themselves, they are more likely to take risks, innovate, and collaborate in meaningful ways. Vulnerability breaks down barriers and builds trust, which is the cornerstone of any thriving relationship or team.

Another key aspect of heart-centered leadership is servant leadership. Instead of viewing leadership as a way to exert control or influence, heart-centered leaders see it as an opportunity to serve others. They focus on how they can uplift and support the people they lead, helping them reach their full potential. This service-oriented approach to leadership shifts the focus from "What can I get?" to "How can I help?" It's about putting the needs of others before your own and leading with a genuine desire to contribute to their success and happiness.

Heart-centered leaders are guided by love, not fear. Fear-based leadership is rooted in control, manipulation, and pressure, but it ultimately leads to a culture of stress, mistrust, and disconnection. In contrast, love-based leadership fosters collaboration, respect, and unity. It creates an environment where people feel safe to express themselves and share their ideas. This type of leadership doesn't diminish accountability or high standards—it simply ensures that those standards are pursued with compassion and understanding.

When you lead with love, you also lead with integrity. Integrity means aligning your actions with your values and doing what's right, even when it's difficult. Heart-centered leaders are guided by a deep sense of purpose and a commitment to making decisions that are in the best interest of the people they lead. They don't cut corners or compromise their values for short-term gain. Instead, they focus on long-term impact and building a legacy of trust, respect, and love.

The ripple effect of heart-centered leadership is powerful. It creates deeper connections, fosters more meaningful relationships, and inspires others to lead with love as well. When people feel supported, valued, and understood, they are more likely to give their best, collaborate effectively, and achieve great things. Heart-centered leadership is a cycle of positive energy that grows stronger as it's shared.

"A great leader breeds more great leaders" - CM

Ask yourself: How can I lead with love today to create deeper, more meaningful connections with the people around me?

Action step: Identify one area in your life—whether it's at work, in a personal relationship, or within your community—where you can practice heart-centered leadership. Focus on leading with empathy, vulnerability, and service in that area. Pay attention to how these qualities deepen your connections with others.

#30 Gratitude as a Superpower:
Flying Above the Bullshit

TONE: Purposeful, Reflective, Empowering, Inspiring, Aspirational

Life is full of challenges. Some are significant, while others are trivial distractions that try to knock us off our path. When you feel like giving up or feel overwhelmed by the weight of it all, you have a choice: you can either fold under pressure or rise above it. Many of the things that challenge us are insignificant in the grand scheme of life, yet they can have a powerful impact if we let them. If you allow the small stuff to knock you off your game, you'll become a victim of the bullshit. Victims fold, complain, and surrender their power to every little inconvenience or challenge that doesn't go their way. But here's the truth: you don't have to live that way.

Gratitude is your superpower, and it's the key to flying above the bullshit that life throws at you. When you choose to adopt an attitude of gratitude, you develop the ability to transcend even the most frustrating situations. The magic of gratitude lies in its ability to shift your perspective from what's going wrong to what's going right. It's a simple yet profound change in focus that allows you to regain your power. Gratitude is like putting on a pair of glasses that let you see the good in every situation, even when things seem chaotic or difficult.

When you embrace gratitude, you move out of victim mode and reclaim control over your attitude and mindset. Victims allow challenges to define them, but grateful people rise above them. They don't get bogged down in trivial annoyances or setbacks because they recognize that these obstacles are temporary and often meaningless in the long run. Gratitude gives you perspective, helping you see beyond the immediate frustration to a bigger picture of growth, opportunity, and progress.

The truth is, life will always challenge you, no matter what stage you're at or how successful you become. The difference between those who fold and those who thrive lies in how they approach these challenges. Those who cultivate gratitude know how to transform obstacles into opportunities. Gratitude turns challenges into stepping stones that lift you higher rather than weighing you down. When you face adversity with gratitude, the very things that could have derailed you become the lessons and experiences that propel you forward.

Gratitude's power comes from its ability to transmute negative energy. Instead of focusing on what's going wrong or feeling defeated, gratitude channels your energy toward what's positive and productive. When you feel grateful for what you have, you naturally attract more of what you want. This doesn't mean pretending challenges don't exist—it means acknowledging them but choosing to focus on the growth, learning, and opportunities that come from those challenges.

Gratitude is especially important when facing small, everyday frustrations. Whether its traffic, a difficult conversation, or a minor setback at work, it's easy to let the little things add up and ruin your day. But when you practice gratitude, these trivial annoyances lose their power. You stop wasting energy on things that don't matter and instead channel that energy toward what's meaningful. Flying above the bullshit means rising above the petty frustrations and keeping your eye on your higher purpose and bigger goals.

Ultimately, gratitude amplifies your personal power. It strengthens your resilience and keeps your energy at a higher frequency. Instead of getting stuck in negativity or complaining about what's wrong, you elevate yourself to a place where you can handle challenges with grace and positivity. Gratitude is what keeps you moving forward when life gets tough, and it's what helps you maintain an empowering attitude when things don't go as planned.

When you commit to gratitude, you'll find that life's challenges no longer feel as heavy. Instead of dragging you down, they become opportunities for growth and learning. Gratitude transforms setbacks into stepping stones, leading you to higher ground. With gratitude as your superpower, you'll find that you're not just surviving life's challenges—you're thriving and soaring above them.

> "Gratitude is not only the greatest of virtues, but the parent of all others."
>
> – Marcus Tullius Cicero

> "Gratitude turns what we have into enough, and more. It turns denial into acceptance, chaos into order, confusion into clarity. It makes sense of our past, brings peace for today, and creates a vision for tomorrow."
>
> – Melody Beattie

> "Gratitude as a starting point will make your actions blessed"
>
> - CM

Ask yourself: How can I use gratitude to rise above the frustrations and challenges in my life right now?

Action step: The next time you feel overwhelmed by a challenge, pause and write down three things you are grateful for about this challenge. Reflect on how those things support you in overcoming the current difficulty. Notice how this practice shifts your energy and helps you see the situation from a higher perspective.

Section 4:

The Journey of Self-Discovery

#31 The Power of Giving Your Best: Building Confidence and Pursuing Your Dreams

TONE: Enlightening, Expansive, Insightful, Reflective, Transformative

The foundation of lifelong happiness begins with being at peace with your decisions. Peace of mind comes from knowing you've done your very best. The guilt and uneasiness that cause average performers to doubt their self-worth often start with a minor decision to quit or not give their full effort. Once you compromise your commitment to giving your best, you begin to lose confidence in yourself.

If you doubt your decisions and your ability to accomplish tasks, you won't have the faith in yourself to pursue your dreams. Without the ability to reach for your dreams, happiness will remain elusive. By always giving your very best, it doesn't matter whether you win or lose—you'll know within yourself that you've done everything you could. The more effort you put into giving your best, the greater your confidence will become.

> **"Believe in yourself! Have faith in your abilities! Without a humble but reasonable confidence in your own powers you cannot be successful or happy"**
>
> **- Norman Vincent Peale**

As your confidence grows, so will your faith in yourself. The stronger your faith in your decisions and actions, the bolder you'll be in pursuing your dreams. The more you attempt to experience your dreams, the happier you'll be.

Average performers are plagued by self-doubt. They question their abilities because of the track record they've established with themselves. They live lives that lack the necessary risks required to grow beyond their fears and achieve their dreams. Champions, on the other hand, always give their best and consistently apply maximum effort, no matter the circumstances.

> **"Conditional happiness or unconditional happiness is a symptom of faith or lack thereof."**
>
> **- CM**

The reward for giving your all is a sense of peace, fulfillment, and pride that leads directly to a happy life.

Ask yourself: Where could I have done more but gave up? Now, forgive yourself and commit to always doing your best.

Action step: Re-commit yourself to a dream or goal that you have given up on. Write down an old goal and reignite your determination to life dream.

#32 Harnessing Intentions:
Realigning Your Power in Times of Change

TONE: Visionary, Aspirational, Reflective, Empowering, Inspirational

In times of rapid change, it's easy to lose sight of where we want to go and what we truly want to achieve. Life can feel like a chaotic pinball machine, with us being bounced around, seemingly without control of the outcome. The world is changing faster than ever, and with so many powerful forces shaping our daily lives, how can we stay in control?

The answer lies in setting clear intentions as a daily ritual. This simple practice can serve as your compass, guiding you to where you want to be. Each day, there are moments when your personal power is at its peak. For some, it's first thing in the morning; for others, it's late at night. It's up to you to discover when you have the most clarity and use that time to set both short-term and long-term intentions.

> **"If you don't have a plan you will default into someone else's plan - CM**

> **"Great Intentions become tragic actions when delivered without careful thought"**
>
> **- Michael Dooley**

As the world around us shifts, we must continually readjust. The difference between those who thrive and those who feel like victims of circumstance is the ability to stay focused on their goals. Life rarely moves in a straight line toward our desires. The universe is constantly in flux, and these fluctuations will inevitably knock you off course. What matters is your ability to readjust, refocus, and reset when those shifts occur.

During times of rapid turbulence, you'll need to rely on your intuition and instincts to guide you. Other times will be quieter—moments of calm when your mind has the space to wander. In those private moments, your imagination will explore both positive and negative possibilities for your future. If you've been habitually setting positive intentions and visualizing a magnificent future for yourself, you'll attract opportunities that lead to your desired outcomes.

However, if you've neglected to condition your thought patterns with intention, the world's programming will take over, and you'll become vulnerable to the influence of others. As humans, we possess the magical gifts of critical thinking, imagination, and the ability to manifest our thoughts into reality. When we harness these gifts, we can live a purposeful, happy, and healthy life. But when we ignore or misuse them, we fall into fear, becoming victims of external forces.

Being a champion of life begins with setting intentions and establishing a daily ritual that realigns your power. When you consciously guide your thoughts, you reclaim control over your destiny.

> **"Sharpen the axe before you cut down the tree"**
>
> **- Marshall Sylver**

Ask yourself: How can I become more intentional about my daily choices?

Action step: Set aside 30 minutes for silent meditation with the intention of visualizing your most magnificent future.

#33 Transformational Experiences: Elevating Awareness and Manifesting Potential

TONE: Thankful, Empowering, Uplifting, Bold, Unshakeable

Anyone committed to personal growth and development understands that one of the key drivers of change is experience. The more heartfelt experiences we live through, the more perspectives we gain, allowing us to interact with reality in deeper, more meaningful ways. However, not all experiences are equal in their transformative power. Often the experiences push us beyond our comfort zones that force us to grow, expanding our awareness and giving us new insights.

"Mastering creation on demand is a result of awareness and vibration." - CM

With an expanded awareness, you begin to perceive your environment with a heightened sense of respect for what's really happening around you. Without awareness, you might overlook something right in front of you—a major character trait, flaw, or hidden potential. It is only through experience that you can become truly aware of the universe around you. The most self-aware individuals didn't get that way by chance. They seek out new experiences with intention, knowing that these adventures will leave them more evolved than when they began.

By consistently and consciously creating new, challenging experiences, you can elevate your awareness to new heights. I believe that at the pinnacle of human potential, we will use our creative abilities to design experiences that drive rapid evolution. The more you know, the more you realize how much you don't know. This expanded awareness and perspective force the mind to ask new questions, and the subconscious will constantly seek answers. To test those answers, new experiences must be created.

The more frequent and intense your experiences, the greater your level of awareness will become. And with greater awareness comes more power to manifest your thoughts into reality. If you aspire to become a master manifester, you can achieve that by raising your Rate of Vibration (ROV). Your ROV increases as you expose yourself to high-frequency, challenging experiences. As your ROV rises, so will your awareness—and, with it, your ability to turn thoughts into things.

One pattern I've observed among those who get the most out of their experiences is a high level of gratitude. People who are genuinely happy, grateful, and thankful for all experiences—even the mundane ones—gain the most value and increase their awareness at the deepest levels. Your attitude toward each experience will determine its ultimate value in your life.

"Transformation literally means going beyond your form"

- Wayne Dyer

Starting any new experience with a clear intention or end goal in mind will compound the positive results, making each moment more impactful.

Ask yourself: Are you engaging in enough transformational experiences to evolve your lifestyle?

Action step: Plan an experience that is outside of your comfort zone. Right before you get started set a clear intention of how you want to be evolved after you are done.

#34 Trusting Your Intuition:
Bold Action, Flow, and the Path to Abundance

TONE: Thankful, Joyful, Positive, Empowering, Uplifting

Taking that first step and showing up is often the hardest part of the journey. The act of consistently taking immediate action on your gut feelings will lead you to new experiences and opportunities. When you follow your intuition and get involved in things that truly resonate with you, you tend to feel more at peace with your life's direction. Second-guessing and regret are negative emotions, and this practice of trusting your instincts will help you become better at making good decisions.

Your initial positive feeling is usually the right one. You are connected to divine, infinite intelligence, and your senses have abilities you may have been restricting or simply unaware of. To fine-tune and calibrate your intuition, you need to consciously act more often on the impulses that come from within. Wayne Gretzky famously said, "You miss 100% of the shots you don't take." So, take more chances and create more momentum in your life. There will be failures along the way, but they are learning opportunities. Don't expect always to be right, because perfection is unattainable. Instead, trust your feelings and listen to your intuition.

> **"Not making a decision is still making a decision. Be bold! Make the call and go with your gut."**
>
> **– CM**

> **"I believe in intuitions and inspirations... I sometimes FEEL that I am right. I do not KNOW that I am."**
>
> **– Albert Einstein**

When you make a wrong call, recognize it, but don't hesitate—keep moving forward. The reality is you will make bad decisions regardless of how careful you are. The goal is to get to a point where you are making spontaneous, correct actions most of the time. By tapping into your connection with infinite intelligence, you will begin to move through life with effortless ease, and more things will start working in your favor as you live in a state of flow.

Failure is part of the journey toward achieving this flow state, so fail forward fast. It's easier to take massive amounts of intuition-driven action quickly and adjust as you go rather than hesitating and acting too slowly. You are capable of spontaneous right action in everything you do, but you need to trust yourself, walk in faith, and not be afraid of failure. Boldness is always rewarded. There is an infinite intelligence speaking to you, and to connect with it, you must step out with faith in yourself and believe that you are capable of making the right decisions in all that you do.

We've all had moments where we made the right call by trusting our intuition, and in those moments, we achieved the best possible outcome. You can make that a permanent part of your life, but it requires bravery and practice. This superpower is within everyone, but you must consciously practice intuitive decision-making until you become unconsciously competent in using it.

It is possible to be in flow with all your actions. The ultimate goal is to become so dialed into this connection with your intuition that your spontaneous right actions guide you and those around you into affluence—a state of abundance where all good things are naturally attracted to you. This includes wealth, good health, positive relationships, and success in every aspect of life.

> **"Following your intuition. That's where true wisdom manifests itself."**
>
> **– Oprah Winfrey**

Ask yourself: Do I allow my intuition to guide me or am I listening to others programming to make my decisions?

Action step: The next 10 times you are faced with making a decision go with your intuition. Make a note about how well it worked and rate your peace of mind as you use this practice.

#35 Emotional Flow:
Releasing Stagnation and Fueling Personal Transformation

TONE: Focused, Immersive, Energizing, Flowing, Empowering

If you dam up water and prevent it from flowing, the water becomes stagnant, stale, rancid, and toxic. Over time, it loses its vitality and turns into something downright unpleasant. The same is true of your emotional energy. When you don't allow your emotions to flow and process naturally, they can fester inside you, poisoning you from within. Just as water purifies itself by flowing freely down a river, your emotional energy must also flow to keep you healthy and balanced.

As your emotional energy flows, it helps cleanse your soul. This process allows you to evolve and grow as you experience the natural highs and lows of life. Life is designed to change you, and your emotional energy is the key to that transformation. Each new experience you encounter, whether positive or negative, offers you an opportunity to process your emotions, learn, and grow.

It's important to remember that emotional stagnation—just like the stagnation of water—leads to toxicity. When we resist our emotions or refuse to process them, they build up, turning into frustration, anxiety, and resentment. Over time, this emotional blockage can lead to a negative mindset and even physical illness. The healthiest way to live is to allow your emotions to flow as they come, just like a river, always moving and purifying itself along the way.

The more you allow yourself to experience life fully, the more you evolve. The natural flow of your emotional energy is tied to the experiences you have, and by opening yourself up to new experiences, you can accelerate your personal growth. In the same way that a river flows faster in a steep canyon, you can speed up your emotional and spiritual evolution by embracing life's challenges and opportunities with a sense of curiosity and adventure.

Water, when it reaches 213 degrees Fahrenheit, boils and turns into steam, transforming from a liquid into a gas. It rises and takes off into the air, leaving behind its old form and becoming something entirely new. What's your boiling point? What level of activity, passion, and engagement do you need in your life to reach that critical temperature where you transform and take off to new heights?

This transformation doesn't happen passively. Just like the water needs heat to reach its boiling point, you need a burning internal desire fueled by passion to reach yours. The more you engage in activities that challenge you, ignite your passion, and push your boundaries, the closer you get to that moment of transformation. It's about living with intensity, being fully present in every moment, and allowing your emotional energy to flow freely toward the life you want to create.

"Emotions at rest get hard like concrete. Expressing your feelings freely creates flow like a thriving river."

– CM

"The soul always knows what to do to heal itself. The challenge is to silence the mind."

– Caroline Myss

Ask yourself: What's holding you back from letting your emotional energy flow? What can you do to engage in more experiences and reach your boiling point of transformation?

Action step: : Identify a conflict or conversation you have been putting off then commit to having that conversation with the intention to have that stagnant energy become something different.

#36 The Power of Surrender: Finding Freedom Through Acceptance

TONE: Liberating, Empowering, Bold, Courageous, Transformative

Struggling against one thing in your life is like struggling against everything. When you manifest a struggle in one area, that energy bleeds into every aspect of your life. This friction creates tension, stress, and unnecessary suffering, blocking you from experiencing the peace and fulfillment you seek. To avoid this unneeded suffering, you must surrender. Surrendering doesn't mean giving up; it means letting go of the need to control every outcome and finding peace in the present moment, no matter the challenges you face.

"If you are to be struggling against anything you are failing in not struggling against everything."
- CM

Acceptance is the key to freedom. When you accept your challenges instead of resisting them, you free yourself from the emotional and mental friction that slows you down. Resistance only amplifies the problem, making it harder to see clearly and find a solution. Acceptance, on the other hand, opens the door to a higher level of thinking. When you stop fighting against your current situation, your mind becomes more open and creative, allowing you to discover the answers and opportunities that were previously hidden by your struggle.

"Surrender to what is. Let go of what was. Have faith in what will be."

– Sonia Ricotti

Surrendering to the present moment does not mean you're giving up on your dreams or aspirations. Instead, it's about owning your problems and accepting 100% responsibility for your current situation. This act of ownership is the first step toward true personal freedom. By acknowledging your role in creating your reality, you empower yourself to make the changes necessary to improve it. You are no longer a victim of circumstance but rather the architect of your life.

Many people live in a constant state of resistance, struggling against their problems and fighting the challenges that come their way. However, this approach only leads to burnout, frustration, and a sense of helplessness. True freedom comes from surrendering to what it is, accepting the challenges as part of the journey, and trusting that within each problem lies a solution. By embracing your situation fully, you gain the clarity and wisdom needed to move forward without the weight of struggle dragging you down.

Owning your problems gives you the power to transform them. When you accept your challenges instead of resisting them, you create space for growth, learning, and progress. This shift in mindset allows you to operate from a place of peace and confidence rather than fear and frustration. Surrender is not about defeat—it's about freedom. It's about releasing the mental chains that bind you and allowing yourself to rise above the struggle.

"The resistance to the unpleasant situation is the root of suffering." – Ram Dass

Ask yourself: In what areas of my life am I resisting, and how can I surrender to these challenges to find clarity and peace?

Action step: Reflect on one area of your life where you feel you are constantly struggling. Take a deep breath and consciously choose to surrender to the situation. Accept it for what it is without resistance, and ask yourself what opportunities for growth or solutions you can see now that you've let go of the need to fight.

<u>#37 The Transformative Power of Experiences: Elevating Awareness and Personal Growth</u>

TONE: Limitless, Bold, Empowering, Visionary, Courageous

Personal growth and development are deeply tied to the experiences we encounter. Every experience offers us a unique opportunity to evolve, but it's the depth and challenge of these experiences that determine how much we grow. The more meaningful and heartfelt the experiences we immerse ourselves in, the greater our awareness becomes. This expanded awareness allows us to interact with reality in new ways, with greater understanding and empathy. Not all experiences are created equal—some may pass by with little impact, while others shake the foundation of who we are, pushing us to reimagine what we know and who we want to become.

"Life long permanent decisions are made during event where the frequencies are amplified"

- CM

Experiences that challenge your comfort zone are the ones that lead to profound growth. When we step into unfamiliar territory, we're forced to question old patterns and stretch our perspectives. It is only through these kinds of experiences that we can truly expand our understanding of the world around us. Think of it like seeing life through a new lens—beforehand, you may have looked at the world but missed critical details, traits, or truths. New experiences reveal those details, expanding your awareness and allowing you to see with clarity what was once invisible.

"When you get into the mix you get mixed into things."

- CM

The most aware and evolved people didn't stumble into that state of mind by accident. They intentionally sought out experiences that would push their limits, expand their minds, and open their hearts. These individuals make a conscious effort to embrace the unfamiliar and set intentions before engaging in new experiences. They understand that growth doesn't come from comfort—it comes from curiosity, challenge, and an openness to what the world has to offer. They move through life with a sense of purpose, using each experience as a tool to elevate their consciousness.

Consistently challenging yourself through new experiences, helps unlock your potential. At the pinnacle of human potential is the realization that we are not just passive participants in life—we are creators of our own evolution. By intentionally seeking out experiences that push our boundaries, we tap into a heightened state of awareness and creativity. The more we expand our awareness, the more we realize how much we still don't know, and this realization ignites a hunger for deeper knowledge and understanding.

"Life is a succession of lessons which must be lived to be understood."

– Ralph Waldo Emerson

This cycle of growth and inquiry doesn't stop. The more you know, the more you want to know. Your subconscious mind, constantly working behind the scenes, seeks out answers to the questions your experiences raise. As you engage in more intense and frequent experiences, your mind and spirit rise to meet those challenges, increasing your ability to manifest your desires into reality. Your rate of vibration (ROV) rises in harmony with the frequency of your experiences, allowing you to align with your dreams and transform your thoughts into things with greater ease.

One pattern I've observed in those who get the most out of their experiences is a profound sense of gratitude. Grateful people are able to extract the value from any experience, even the seemingly mundane. They approach life with an appreciation for the journey, recognizing that every experience—good or bad—offers an opportunity for growth and increased awareness. Attitude shapes experience, and those who enter new experiences with an open mind and a grateful heart tend to evolve more rapidly.

When you set intentions before any new experience, you create a framework for transformation. With each experience, ask yourself: What can I learn? How can this challenge or new situation help me grow? This mindset creates a ripple effect, where one positive experience builds on the next, leading to exponential personal growth.

> **"The only source of knowledge is experience." – Albert Einstein**

Ask yourself: Am I actively seeking out transformative experiences, or am I stuck in my comfort zone, missing opportunities to evolve?

Action step: Commit to seeking out one new experience each week that challenges your comfort zone. Reflect on what you learned and how it expanded your awareness. Approach each experience with gratitude, and watch how your perspective on life transforms.

#38 The Mastery of Challenges: Embracing Growth Through Adversity

TONE: Visionary, Creative, Purposeful, Motivational, Aspirational

Lifestyle masters view challenges as opportunities for growth. Rather than avoiding adversity or shrinking in the face of difficulty, they see every challenge as a chance to elevate themselves. By consistently tackling challenges head-on, you develop a higher tolerance for difficulty and push yourself toward mastery. Average people, when confronted with challenges, tend to retreat or avoid the discomfort that comes with them. But those who master their lives understand that every challenge conquered builds a foundation of strength, resilience, and confidence.

> **"Trying to shortcut your challenges will only delay your dreams"**
>
> **- CM**

Overcoming challenges is not about brute strength alone—it's about persistence, consistency, enthusiasm, and willpower. Every challenge you face and conquer adds another layer to your confidence. With each victory, the next obstacle feels smaller, more manageable, and less intimidating. The more challenges you overcome, the braver you become in pursuing your heart's desires. Challenges, in fact, are often less difficult than they appear. It's the anticipation of struggle that magnifies the fear, but once you decide to face the challenge, you find that solutions reveal themselves naturally.

> **"Strength does not come from winning. Your struggles develop your strengths."**
>
> **– Arnold Schwarzenegger**

The decision to embrace adversity is often the turning point in overcoming it. Once you commit to facing a challenge, the universe has a way of aligning with your intention, presenting you with opportunities and answers. More often than not, your subconscious mind already holds the solutions to many of your problems. However, it's not until you fully embrace the challenge and make a conscious decision to tackle it that your subconscious mind's brilliance emerges.

The world's greatest achievements often come from individuals or small groups who face enormous challenges and conquer them step by step. These people build their confidence by overcoming one difficulty after another in a sequential order, tackling one seemingly impossible task at a time. By breaking down massive challenges into smaller, more manageable pieces, you can begin to chip away at even the most daunting obstacles. This methodical approach will lead you to mastery—not only of the challenges themselves but also of your ability to handle adversity with grace.

To fully master your lifestyle, you must develop the confidence to face any obstacle and get the results necessary to achieve your dreams. Challenges are not barriers to your success; they are stepping-stones on the path to becoming a stronger, more capable version of yourself. Each challenge is an opportunity for growth, and with every obstacle you overcome, you are one step closer to living the life of your dreams.

"Challenges are what make life interesting; overcoming them is what makes life meaningful."

– Joshua J. Marine

Ask yourself: How can I reframe the challenges in my life as opportunities to grow and build confidence?

Action step: Identify a challenge in your life that you've been avoiding. Break it down into smaller, more manageable steps. Tackle one step at a time, and as you complete each task, notice how your confidence grows. Use that momentum to take on the next part of the challenge.

#39 Uncovering Your Authentic Self: The Power of Knowing Who You Are

TONE: Empowering, Focused, Determined, Bold, Optimistic

In a world where we're constantly bombarded with external influences, it's easy to lose sight of who we truly are. From social expectations, family pressures, and the endless noise of media, many of us spend years trying to conform to ideals that are not our own. But true happiness, fulfillment, and success come from knowing and embracing your authentic self. When you understand who you are at your core, you unlock a power that allows you to live with purpose, confidence, and joy.

> "Authenticity is rare. When you encounter real ass people go the extra mile to create a relationship and be memorable"
>
> - CM

Uncovering your authentic self is the process of stripping away the layers of conditioning, fear, and expectation that have been placed on you. It's about getting back to the essence of who you were before the world told you who to be. It's not always an easy journey, but it's one of the most rewarding and transformative experiences you can have.

The first step in uncovering your authentic self is self-awareness. This means taking a deep and honest look at your life, your choices, and your patterns. What motivates you? What brings you joy? What are your strengths, passions, and values? Too often, we live on autopilot, following routines and habits that don't reflect who we truly are. Self-awareness is about waking up to your own life and realizing that you have the power to shape it in a way that aligns with your deepest desires and true nature.

One of the biggest barriers to uncovering your authentic self is fear—fear of judgment, fear of rejection, and fear of the unknown. We often conform to what others expect because it feels safer. But living for others means sacrificing the unique gifts and perspectives that make you who you are. Embracing your authentic self requires courage—the courage to step away from external validation and to trust that who you are is enough. It's about letting go of the need to be liked or accepted by everyone and finding peace in being true to yourself.

Authenticity is not about perfection. It's about honesty. It's about embracing your imperfections, your vulnerabilities, and your unique quirks. When you are authentic, you no longer feel the need to put on a mask or pretend to be someone you're not. You allow yourself to be fully seen, and in doing so, you attract deeper and more meaningful connections with others. People are drawn to authenticity because it's rare and refreshing in a world that often encourages conformity.

Knowing who you are also means having a strong sense of your values. Your values are your guiding principles—the things that matter most to you in life. When you live in alignment with your values, you feel more grounded and centered, even when challenges arise. Your decisions become easier because you have a clear understanding of what's most important to you. Conversely, when you live out of alignment with your values, you feel disconnected and dissatisfied, even if everything looks "right" on the surface.

The beauty of uncovering your authentic self is that it unlocks your potential. When you know who you are, you stop wasting energy trying to fit into someone else's mold. You can focus your energy on pursuing your passions, achieving your goals, and living a life that feels true to you. Authenticity brings a sense of freedom and empowerment that allows you to take bold steps toward your dreams. You're no longer held back by fear or doubt because you trust in your own path.

It's also important to recognize that uncovering your authentic self is an ongoing process. As you grow and evolve, your understanding of who you are may change. This is natural. The key is to stay connected to yourself, continually checking in with your thoughts, feelings, and desires. The more you practice self-awareness, the more deeply you will connect with your authentic self, and the more fully you will be able to live out your purpose.

"The privilege of a lifetime is to become who you truly are."

– Carl Jung

"To be yourself in a world that is constantly trying to make you something else is the greatest accomplishment."

– Ralph Waldo Emerson

Ask yourself: Am I living in alignment with my true self, or am I trying to meet the expectations of others? What outside influences am I trying to live up to?

Action step: Take some time to reflect on who you truly are by journaling. Write down your core values, passions, and the activities that make you feel most alive. Then, identify one area in your life where you're not living authentically and take one small step toward aligning that area with your true self.

#40 Becoming Your Future Self: Envisioning and Channeling Your Best Version

TONE: Abundant, Empowering, Prosperous, Visionary, Motivational

There is extreme power in learning how to channel the most magnificent version of your future self. Channeling, in this context, is when you connect to the spirit of something beyond your present self and embrace its perspective and qualities. When you channel your future self, you are connecting to a version of yourself that you can consciously influence and shape into something positive, powerful, and inspiring. This process allows you to access the traits, attitudes, and behaviors that will define the best version of yourself, even before you fully embody them.

> "When you make you very best friend the most magnificent versions of your future self you will always have someone to guide you to the best answers" - CM

To envision your future self, it starts with dreaming up the qualities and attributes you most admire. Who do you want to become? What kind of person do you want to be? Begin by defining the traits—such as resilience, confidence, kindness, wisdom, and creativity—that your future self-embodies. This is where your imagination becomes your most powerful tool. You can create the ultimate version of yourself, and by consistently channeling this future self, you start to become that person today.

Surrounding yourself with greatness is one of the most effective ways to fuel your vision of your future self. Reading stories of great leaders, thinkers, and innovators helps you to understand the qualities that have shaped them. Spending time with inspiring people, those who live boldly and with purpose elevates your thinking and expands your sense of what's possible. When you immerse yourself in environments filled with dynamic problem solvers, trailblazers, and risk-takers, you're pushed out of your comfort zone—and this is where character is forged.

It's important to remember that building character isn't about choosing the easy path. The experiences that shape the richest character often come from the hardest challenges. Growth doesn't happen when life is smooth and simple; it happens in the fires of difficulty, sacrifice, hardship, and perseverance. When you face struggle head-on, when you endure pain and sorrow, you're not only building strength but also depth and wisdom. The struggle itself is the teacher, and those who embrace it are the ones who grow into the greatest versions of themselves.

While imagining your future self is a powerful tool, the experiences that force you to grow truly solidify this transformation. Reading about someone else's struggle can provide perspective, but nothing compares to living it. When you personally experience fear, danger, and challenge, you gain a firsthand understanding of how to overcome it. This is the foundation of character, and it is through these lived experiences that you channel the essence of your future self-more deeply.

Humanity has learned through struggle, and it's this ability to persevere in the face of danger, hardship, and uncertainty that has made our species great. Throughout history, humans have faced and overcome tremendous obstacles, from surviving natural disasters to thriving in the face of war and famine. Our greatness lies in our ability to rise, even when the odds are against us. When you tap into this legacy of resilience, you understand that you, too, are capable of incredible feats of strength and growth.

By channeling the lessons of those who came before you, along with your own personal struggles, you are able to use these insights to fuel your vision of your future self. When you face your own challenges, think about how your future self would handle the situation. Would they be calm under pressure? Would they have the wisdom to navigate through it? With each decision, you are moving closer either to becoming your best self or away from it. Every choice you make shapes the future version of you.

The process of becoming your future self requires you to take bold steps toward growth. It means constantly pushing yourself outside of your comfort zone, confronting fear, and embracing opportunities for development. The more you experience and learn, the more you grow into your future self—the person who embodies everything you admire, respect, and aspire to be. Your future self is not a distant concept; it's waiting for you to claim it with each action you take today.

By consistently channeling your future self, you manifest a version of yourself that not only achieves personal greatness but also inspires others around you. You create a legacy that your family, friends, and community will be proud of. A future self is not someone you hope to be "someday"—this is the self you are actively becoming right now.

> **"The best way to predict the future is to create it."**
>
> **– Peter Drucker**

Ask yourself: Am I living in alignment with my true self, or am I trying to meet the expectations of others? What outside influences am I trying to live up to?

Action step: Take a moment to write a detailed description of your future self. Include the traits, habits, attitudes, and qualities that this version of you embodies. Reflect on this vision daily and take one action today that aligns you with your future self. Whether it's making a decision with greater wisdom or handling a challenge with calm, let your future self-guide your present actions

<u>Section 5:</u>

<u>Building Meaningful Relationships</u>

#41 The Pillars of Relationships: Trust, Respect, and the Path to Healing

TONE: Uplifting, Challenging, Encouraging, Resilient, Determined

Every relationship in your life will either succeed or fail based on trust and respect. If a healthy relationship becomes damaged, it is usually due to a breach of trust or a loss of respect. When trust is broken, the relationship becomes burdened with processes that limit the happiness it can generate. Without complete trust, the heart and mind restrict their ability to fully engage. As a self-defense mechanism, our innate intelligence creates barriers to protect us from untrustworthy energy.

"Shredding your ego through love trust and respect for yourself is the direct path to happiness and lifestyle mastery" - CM

Emotional and mental healing rooted in love must occur to restore trust before the soul can fully re-engage with someone who has violated it. Sometimes this healing never happens, as it requires both parties to forgive and evolve beyond the damage.

When respect is damaged or lost, the relationship suffers because there is a misalignment in moral values. A relationship cannot flourish without compassion and empathy toward another person's perspective. It is not necessary to share the same beliefs to thrive together, but respect for each other's beliefs is essential.

In any relationship, it's natural not to always see eye to eye, and that's okay. However, if you cannot respect how the other person arrived at their viewpoint, the relationship will never reach its full potential. By dissolving your ego and the need to be right, you become more tolerant of different ideas. With an open mind, you can honor others for who they are, free of judgment. This creates space for genuine respect.

You can only receive respect to the extent that you give it. By loving, trusting, and respecting yourself fully, you create the opportunity for your relationships to reach their highest potential.

"Trust is earned, respect is given and loyalty is demonstrated. Betrayal of any one of these three is a loss of all." - Unknown

Ask yourself: What important relationship in my life can be improved by intentionally repairing the trust and respect levels?

Action step: Identify a relationship in your life that is sub-optimal and set a meeting with that person. During the meeting do your best to restore trust and respect to 100% for both of you.

<u>#42 The Power of Creation: Manifesting Ideas into Reality</u>

TONE: Action-Oriented, Bold, Confident, Energizing, Inspiring

Turning ideas into reality is the ultimate act of service. Humans possess the extraordinary ability to transform thoughts into tangible things. Nothing else in the universe, as far as we know, has the creative power that we do. Ideas are gifts from divine intelligence, a source we are all connected to. This divine intelligence is all-knowing and has unlimited potential to inspire our imagination. However, it relies on us to bring these ideas into existence.

"The true sign of intelligence is not knowledge but imagination"

- Albert Einstein

The divine can envision, but it requires the mind and body to bring those visions to life. The mind needs education, logic, emotion, willpower, creativity, and other attributes to propel the body into action. The body, in turn, needs nourishment, energy, health, balance, and other essentials to carry out those actions. Together, the spirit, mind, and body create a powerful connection that allows us to manifest.

"Heart centered creation is the pinnacle of human existence"

- CM

Our ability to create is our greatest contribution to existence. The more heart-centered, purpose-driven ideas we bring into the physical world, the more we thrive as a species. This includes creating art, music, love, and anything that enriches life. The potential for sophistication in our creations is infinite. Progress and evolution of our ideas are the natural course of expansion. A great idea will flourish if the mind and body are properly fueled.

The bigger the problem, the more advanced our creations must become. We are all creators, but not everyone is creating with purpose or awareness.

Ask yourself: What am I proud of creating, and how does it serve others?

Action step: Think of someone in your life you'd like to support. Then imagine a kind act of service that could make their life better. Use your creativity to make it happen and show them that they are special and that you care.

#43 Pushing Beyond Your Best:
The Path to Excellence and Gratitude

TONE: Instinctual, Trusting, Flowing, Grounded, Empowered

Always do your best! No matter what you're engaged in, strive to give your very best effort. Living your best life begins with the decision to execute with excellence. When you think you're doing your best, stop and ask yourself, "How can I do better?" Always aim to surpass your current best. It might feel awkward or unnatural at first, but the consistent practice of pushing yourself will start to feel more natural over time.

If you're a kind person, strive to be even kinder. If you're a hard worker, aim to become an even better one. There is always room for improvement, and with an attitude of continuous self-betterment, you can be more, achieve more, earn more, and ultimately experience greater happiness.

By being grateful for the opportunity to improve, you'll generate the focus and energy needed to elevate your performance. The work may not always be glorious or fun—it might even be something you dislike—but do whatever it takes to get where you want to go. We all have to make sacrifices to achieve greatness.

What separates world-class champions from the average person is their willingness to tackle the hard, unglamorous work with full commitment. Champions turn their attitude into gratitude and treat every breath as a gift from God. They honor their time alive by giving the world more than their best.

What you will discover is a reward that you could never have possibly imagined.

"When the road is difficult, times are hard and path is uncertain you can always find peace knowing you did your best" - CM

"To give anything less than your best is to sacrifice your best"

- Legendary Runner Steve Prefontain

"The goal is not to be better than the other man but to be better than your previous self"

- The Dalai Lama

Ask yourself: In what ways can I be better at a thing that I am already really good at?

Action step: During a job or task that you don't like doing, convert your attitude to gratitude and a give a "better than your best" effort with no expectation of any additional reward.

#44 Embracing Imperfection:
Transforming Guilt, Releasing Shame, and Finding Empowerment

TONE: Hopeful, Empowering, Collaborative, Expansive, Visionary

We all make mistakes. We've all done things we regret, but how we deal with those mistakes determines the results we attract in the future. You can look at the problems you've created and choose to feel disempowered, or you can choose to be empowered. You can lie to yourself, saying that your problems make you less worthy, or you can lie and say they make you more worthy. Either way, you're telling yourself a story. So, choose the story that empowers you and avoid the one that weakens you.

Guilt and shame can drain your energy and hold you down, but understanding the difference between them will help you process your emotions and move into a space of positive creation.

Guilt and shame are not the same. Guilt is recognizing that you've done something wrong and knowing you can do better. Shame, on the other hand, is internalizing those feelings and telling yourself, "I am a bad person." Don't allow shame to become part of your identity. You are better without it.

Release the shame and forgive yourself. Accept that life isn't perfect, and neither are you. Surrender to that imperfection and find the beauty in it—because life is perfect as it is.

"Unlike guilt which is the feeling of doing something wrong, shame is the feeling of being something wrong"

- Marilyn J Sorensen

"You either walk inside your story and own it or hustle outside your story for your worthiness"

- Brené Brown

"Surrender and find your life perfect" - CM

Ask yourself: What shame am I holding, and how can I find forgiveness to create empowering feelings instead?

Action step: Surender and find your life perfect.

#45 Rise Above Victimhood:
Embrace Responsibility and Become a Champion of Your Destiny

TONE: Attentive, Compassionate, Thoughtful, Engaging, Warm, Visionary

In today's world, victim mentality seems to be more rewarded than ever. We see people protesting for equal rights and blaming others for the injustices they experience. This behavior has become popular, and, in many cases, it seems to be validated by society. Taking personal responsibility for one's life, on the other hand, is seen as difficult, even when some of the wealthiest and most influential individuals claim victimhood based on race, history, or circumstance. The truth is that people are often rewarded for choosing to view themselves as victims of society.

> "Victim mentality is programmed. Programs can easily be deleted or rewritten"
>
> - CM

But this mindset comes with a cost. When we see ourselves as victims, we give away our power to create change in our lives. Instead of taking control, we allow external circumstances to dictate our fate. It's time to change this paradigm. It's time to rise up as champions of our own destinies and reject the idea of victimhood.

Victim mentality breeds envy, and envy leads to plunder. Plunder happens when people feel entitled to what others have earned and demand more than what they contribute. This creates a system where consumption exceeds production, leading to collapse. Are you guilty of contributing to this cycle of plunder? Are you part of the disease of victimhood that is draining the producers of this world of what they've worked hard to create?

There's a better way forward—a way that allows you to take control of your own destiny instead of blaming others for what you lack. The first step is to stop seeing yourself as a victim and start embracing personal responsibility. When you take ownership of your life, you begin to realize that your actions, your decisions, and your mindset are what ultimately shape your future.

In the future, make a pledge to produce more than you consume. Commit to contributing more than you take. Stop looking at others who have earned more and envying their success. Instead, focus on building your own path to success. When you stop viewing yourself as a victim, you free yourself from the limitations that come with that mindset. You open yourself up to the possibility of becoming producer—a person who adds value to the world and takes responsibility for their own life. It's time to stop being fooled into thinking you are powerless. You have the ability to shape your future and create a life that is defined by your choices, not by the circumstances you were born into. Take charge, rise above victimhood, and become the champion of your own destiny.

Ask yourself: In what ways do I act like a victim? empowering feelings instead?

Action step: Attend a social event as a champion and produce something special for the event or other guests. Produce more than you consume and seek no recognition for your contribution.

#46 Empowered Spirit:
Manifesting a Future of Passion and Purpose

TONE: Consistent, Persistent, Structured, Empowering, Rewarding, Warm, Visionary

With an empowered spirit, one can envision a future filled with joy, passion, and purpose. This vision, this dream of what can be, will guide your actions and lead you to your destiny. The path to your most magnificent future is already laid out before you—waiting for you to follow your heart's desires. But the journey requires more than just ambition; it demands faith in the unknown and trust in the divine compass that guides you.

Faith is the key to steering you away from fear and toward the warm embrace of your true purpose. Along the way, there will be many external influences—doubt, fear, and the pressures of society—that will try to pull you away from your vision. However, these distractions can only succeed if you allow them to. You must keep your inner light, the flame of your passion, burning brightly. That flame will guide you through every challenge and obstacle that appears in your path.

To reach your ultimate future, you must believe in it with every fiber of your being and fuel it with a burning desire. Your heart already knows the way, but you must nurture the passion and enthusiasm necessary for the journey. New levels of consistency, persistence, and love will need to be discovered and developed to achieve the breakthroughs that will lead you toward your greatest achievements.

> "Make your very best friend the most magnificent version of your future self. You can ask your future self questions and get answers that will bring you closer to your best self"
>
> - CM

> "Believe in yourself and all that you are. Know that there is something inside you that is greater than any obstacle." – Christian D. Larson

Your future may look different from anything that's been done before. To reach such heights, you will need to think and act in new ways—guided by love, creativity, and faith. You are the dreamer and the architect of your own life. As such, you must empower your spirit to dream boldly and pursue that dream with relentless determination.

Belief in yourself is not just important—it's essential. While it feels special when others believe in you, the most critical belief must come from within. It's your belief in your own potential, your limitless abilities, and your capacity to shape your future that will carry you forward. You are powerful beyond measure, and with faith in yourself, you will manifest the future you desire.

> "Faith is taking the first step even when you don't see the whole staircase." – Martin Luther King Jr

> **Ask yourself:** How can I add more passion and emotion to my vision of the future?

> **Action step:** Close your eyes and envision your ideal future in vivid detail. How does it feel? What does it look like? Write down three small steps you can take today to move toward that vision, and commit to one actionable step right now

#47 The Art of Deep Listening:
Strengthening Bonds Through Presence

TONE: Purposeful, Compassionate, Empowering, Driven, Visionary

In a world filled with constant distractions, it can be difficult to be truly present in our interactions with others. The art of deep listening is one of the most powerful tools for building meaningful connections and strengthening bonds with the people in our lives. Deep listening goes beyond simply hearing the words someone is saying—it's about being fully present, tuning into their emotions, and giving them your undivided attention. When you listen deeply, you show the other person that you value their thoughts and feelings, and this creates a foundation of trust and understanding.

> **"The art of listening is a skill that requires practice and reflection."**
>
> **- CM**

At its core, deep listening is about presence. It requires you to put aside your own thoughts, opinions, and distractions to focus entirely on the person in front of you. This isn't always easy in a world where we're constantly bombarded with notifications, responsibilities, and mental chatter. But when you commit to listening deeply, you create a space where the other person feels truly heard. Presence means being in the moment, not thinking about what you're going to say next, not glancing at your phone, and not getting lost in your own thoughts. It's about giving your full attention and energy to the conversation.

> **"Most people do not listen with the intent to understand; they listen with the intent to reply."**
>
> **– Stephen R. Covey**

Deep listening strengthens bonds because it fosters genuine connection. When someone feels heard and understood, they naturally open up more, trust more, and feel safer sharing their true selves. This is especially important in close relationships—whether with family, friends, or partners—where deep listening can deepen intimacy and build a stronger emotional connection. By listening with an open heart and mind, you create an environment where people feel safe to express their thoughts, emotions, and vulnerabilities without fear of judgment or dismissal.

Listening deeply also requires empathy. It's not enough to simply understand the words being spoken—you need to tune into the emotions behind those words. What is the other person really trying to convey? How do they feel about what they're saying? Empathy allows you to connect with their emotional state and respond in a way that makes them feel supported. By listening for what's unsaid, you demonstrate that you care about their feelings, not just the facts of what they're communicating.

One of the challenges of deep listening is the natural urge to interject with your own thoughts or solutions. Often, when someone shares a problem or a difficult experience, our first instinct is to offer advice or relate it to something we've experienced. While these responses come from a place of care, they can sometimes disrupt the flow of the conversation and shift the focus away from the speaker's needs. Deep listening involves resisting the urge to fix, solve, or respond right away. Sometimes, what the other person needs most is simply to be heard. Listening without an agenda allows you to truly understand their perspective and fosters a deeper connection.

Another key aspect of deep listening is nonverbal communication. Listening is not just about your ears—it involves your whole body. Eye contact, nodding, leaning in, and maintaining an open posture all signal that you are fully engaged in the conversation. Your body language should match your intention to be present. These small gestures show that you are focused and invested in the other person's words and emotions. Additionally, silence plays a powerful role in deep listening. Allowing pauses and silence creates space for the other person to reflect and fully express themselves without feeling rushed.

Deep listening transforms relationships. When practiced consistently, it strengthens bonds, builds trust, and fosters mutual understanding. People remember how you make them feel, and when they feel truly heard, it creates a lasting impact. Whether you're resolving a conflict, offering support, or simply having a casual conversation, deep listening can turn everyday interactions into moments of connection. It shows that you care, that you value the other person's experience, and that you're willing to be fully present with them, even in the midst of a busy world.

Ask yourself: How can I practice deep listening in my relationships to create deeper connections and build more trust?

Action step: In your next conversation, practice deep listening by focusing solely on the other person. Put away your phone, make eye contact, and listen without interrupting. Pay attention to their emotions, and resist the urge to offer advice or solutions unless they ask. Reflect on how this changes the quality of the conversation and strengthens your connection.

#48 From Surface to Substance: Building Relationships That Matter

TONE: Optimistic, Uplifting, Empowering, Energizing, Joyful, Visionary

In a world where social media, texting, and quick exchanges dominate our interactions, it's easy to maintain relationships that exist on the surface. We scroll through pictures, exchange a few words, and check in just enough to stay in each other's lives. But when it comes to truly meaningful relationships, substance is what makes the difference. Building relationships that matter requires depth, intention, and a genuine connection. To move from surface-level interactions to substantive, fulfilling relationships, we need to focus on cultivating trust, vulnerability, and presence.

"Resonating on the same vibe for an extended amount of time will build a report that will endure hardships." - CM

Surface relationships are easy to maintain because they don't require much emotional investment. They often involve casual conversations, light topics, and minimal vulnerability. While these relationships can serve a purpose—such as maintaining acquaintances or networking—they rarely offer the deep sense of fulfillment that comes from truly meaningful connections. Relationships of substance require effort, but they also offer greater rewards: trust, understanding, mutual support, and a shared sense of purpose.

The first step in building substantial relationships is being intentional about how you engage with others. It's not enough to exchange pleasantries or chat about surface-level topics. You need to be willing to go deeper, to ask thoughtful questions, and to show a genuine interest in the other person's thoughts, feelings, and experiences. When you take the time to listen deeply, you create space for others to share their true selves. This opens the door to deeper conversations that build trust and foster connection.

Vulnerability is another key ingredient in meaningful relationships. People often keep their guard up, presenting only the parts of themselves they feel are "safe" to share. But to build relationships that matter, you must be willing to show up authentically—even when it feels uncomfortable. Vulnerability creates intimacy. It signals to others that you trust them enough to share your true self, including your challenges, fears, and imperfections. When you allow yourself to be vulnerable, you give others permission to do the same, and this shared authenticity strengthens the bond between you.

One of the most important aspects of moving from surface to substance is trust. Trust is the foundation of all meaningful relationships, and it's built over time through consistent, honest, and open communication. Trust develops when both people feel safe enough to be themselves without fear of judgment or rejection. This means showing up for each other, keeping your word, and being reliable. When trust is present, you can navigate challenges, disagreements, and difficult conversations with respect and understanding. Trust transforms relationships from casual connections to meaningful partnerships.

Another way to add substance to your relationships is to invest time and energy into them. Substantial relationships don't happen by accident; they require intentional effort. This means making time to connect regularly, whether through phone calls, in-person meetings, or meaningful messages. It's about prioritizing the relationship and showing that you value it enough to nurture its growth. When you invest time in someone, you demonstrate that they are important to you, which in turn deepens the relationship and creates a stronger bond.

Shared experiences also play a significant role in building relationships that matter. These can range from working together on a project, facing a challenge side by side, or simply spending quality time together. When you share meaningful experiences, you create memories and a sense of camaraderie that strengthens your connection. Shared experiences are the glue that binds relationships and helps them grow deeper over time.

Finally, meaningful relationships require presence. In today's busy world, it's easy to be physically present but mentally elsewhere. To build deep relationships, you need to be fully engaged in the moment when you're with someone. This means putting away distractions, like your phone or work, and giving the other person your undivided attention. Presence signals respect and care. It shows the other person that they are worth your time and attention, and this fosters trust and connection on a deeper level.

By focusing on these key elements—intention, vulnerability, trust, time, shared experiences, and presence—you can transform your relationships from surface-level interactions to ones filled with substance and meaning. These are the relationships that matter, the ones that bring you joy, support, and fulfillment.

> **"True friendship comes when the silence between two people is comfortable."**
>
> **– David Tyson**

Ask yourself: How can I bring more substance into my relationships and create deeper connections with the people who matter most to me?

Action step: Identify one relationship in your life that feels surface-level, and make an intentional effort to deepen it. Start by asking more meaningful questions, showing vulnerability, or planning a shared experience that will strengthen your bond. Notice how the relationship evolves when you focus on substance rather than surface.

#49 Partying to Prosperity:
Bonding Through Good Times with Your Squad

TONE: Energizing, Grounding, Elevated, Purposeful Joyful Visionary, Rewarding

Humans are, at our core, social creatures. From the earliest days of humanity, we've thrived in groups—whether it was for survival, companionship, or the sheer joy of celebration. Being part of a squad, a community, or a close-knit group has always been an essential element of the human experience. In fact, some of the most memorable moments in life are those shared with friends and family, celebrating victories, milestones, or just the beauty of life itself. Building strong bonds with others is the foundation of prosperity, both in personal fulfillment and in external success.

> **"Partying as an art form is not only entertainment at its finest, it is friendship magic at its finest."**
>
> **- CM**

In today's fast-paced, tech-driven world, however, building and maintaining meaningful connections has become more challenging. The rise of technology and the constant barrage of media have created barriers between us and those around us. With smartphones, social media, and a never-ending stream of news and entertainment, it's easy to become disconnected from the real-world interactions that once defined our relationships. While these tools were meant to bring us closer, they often leave us more isolated, scrolling through feeds instead of building deeper bonds.

> **"Prosperity is not just about money; it's about the richness of your relationships."**
>
> **– Unknown**

One of the reasons for this disconnection is the media's focus on negativity. Bad news sells. Whether it's stories of conflict, danger, or division, negative news captures our attention because of our natural survival instincts. Since ancient times, humans have had to pay close attention to threats in order to survive. Media outlets know this, and they exploit it to keep us glued to their content. Fear, danger, and controversy flood our screens, making us more wary of others, fueling distrust, and, ultimately, keeping us from forming genuine connections.

This constant stream of negativity can make it harder to build relationships, but here's the truth: real prosperity comes from connection. The things you want in life—whether it's happiness, wealth, freedom, or success—will often come from other people. That's why it's so important to create spaces where you can bond deeply with your squad, free of distractions and negativity. Parties, celebrations, and shared experiences are powerful tools for doing just that. When you get together with your friends and family to celebrate, you're not just having a good time—you're building community, strengthening relationships, and feeding your soul.

Celebrations aren't just fun; they're essential. They remind us of our shared humanity, allow us to express gratitude for each other, and create lasting memories that deepen our connections. Whether it's a small gathering or a large event, intentional celebrations foster camaraderie, trust, and joy. These are the moments that bind us together, and through these bonds, we create networks of support that lead to true prosperity.

Prosperity comes in many forms. It might be financial wealth, but it can also be the wealth of friendships, freedom, love, or opportunities. And often, the best way to tap into that prosperity is by strengthening the connections you have with others. The people in your life are your greatest asset, and the more you invest time and energy into building those relationships, the more you'll find that prosperity naturally flows into your life. Think of it this way: the people you surround yourself with can open doors, provide support, and help you achieve your dreams. But these benefits only come when there's a real bond of trust and friendship.

One of the most powerful ways to create those bonds is through shared celebrations and rituals. Whether you're marking a major achievement, celebrating a birthday, or just getting together for the sake of it, these gatherings create an environment where relationships can flourish. When people come together to celebrate, they're not just marking the occasion—they're creating a sacred bond, a sense of unity that strengthens the group and uplifts the human spirit. This is why celebrations are often at the heart of prosperity, especially after major achievements like a championship win or a business success. The shared joy creates a lasting bond that makes future victories even more meaningful.

In a world that often emphasizes individual success, it's easy to forget the power of community. But true success is rarely achieved alone. The more you connect with others—especially in positive, intentional environments—the more you'll realize how much you gain from being part of something bigger than yourself. Celebrating life with your squad not only enhances your sense of fulfillment, but it also strengthens the connections that will help you prosper in every area of your life.

So, whether it's throwing a party, hosting a family gathering, or simply celebrating small wins with your friends, remember that prosperity and connection go hand in hand. The more you invest in your relationships, the more you'll create a life that's rich in joy, support, and success.

Ask yourself: How can I create more opportunities to celebrate life and strengthen my connections with the people who matter most?

Action step: Plan a celebration with your closest friends or family, whether it's for a special occasion or just to enjoy each other's company. Make it intentional—focus on being fully present and creating memories. Reflect on how this gathering strengthens your bond with those around you.

#50 The Greatest Community: Demonstrating Selfless Compassion

TONE: Resilient, Bold, Unstoppable, Courageous, Empowering, Joyful

The true measure of any community lies in the depth of its empathy and compassion. A community where people genuinely care for each other, where selflessness is not the exception but the rule, is one that creates an atmosphere of joy, belonging, and peace. When you're part of a community that puts others first, it's like experiencing heaven on earth. It's a place where thoughtfulness and kindness flow freely, where support is given without hesitation, and where everyone is uplifted by the collective spirit of service and love.

> **"For a happy life produce for your community more than you consume."**
>
> **- CM**

At the heart of a selfless community is the belief that giving is more fulfilling than receiving. Selfless compassion means putting aside your own needs and desires to focus on the well-being of others. This doesn't mean neglecting yourself, but rather recognizing that when you lift others up, you also elevate yourself. True fulfillment comes from service, from knowing that you've contributed to someone else's happiness, comfort, or success. And the beautiful thing about a compassionate community is that the giving is mutual—when everyone is focused on helping each other, the cycle of generosity continues to grow, creating an environment of abundance and care.

Compassion can only be fully experienced through action. It's one thing to feel empathy for someone or to think kind thoughts, but it's an entirely different thing to take action that improves someone's life. Compassion requires stepping outside of yourself, engaging with others, and making a conscious decision to serve. Generous service is what transforms empathy into tangible love, and when you witness acts of selflessness within a community, it ignites your own compassion, deepening your connection to those around you.

In a selfless community, people actively seek out ways to support each other. Whether it's lending a helping hand, offering a kind word, or simply being there in times of need, these small gestures of compassion make a profound impact. And it's not just about helping when it's convenient—true compassion is most powerful when it's given without expecting anything in return. It's about giving for the sake of giving, knowing that the act itself is its own reward.

> **"The best way to find yourself is to lose yourself in the service of others."**
>
> **– Mahatma Gandhi**

Witnessing thoughtfulness and selflessness in others can also inspire you to become more compassionate. When you see someone go out of their way to help, or when you experience kindness firsthand, it creates a ripple effect. You become more attuned to the needs of others, more willing to lend a hand, and more motivated to contribute to the well-being of the community. This is the beauty of selfless compassion—it's contagious. One act of kindness can inspire another, and before long, the entire community is transformed by a spirit of giving.

The power of selfless compassion lies not only in what it does for others but also in what it does for you. When you give from the heart, without expectation, you experience a sense of fulfillment and purpose that can't be found through self-serving actions. You develop a deeper understanding of what it means to be human, to be part of something greater than yourself. Service to others feeds the soul, and the more you give, the more your own capacity for love and empathy grows.

A compassionate community also fosters a sense of belonging. When you're surrounded by people who care, who are there to support you without judgment or expectation, you feel safe and valued. This sense of belonging creates a foundation of trust and security that allows everyone to thrive. In this type of environment, people feel more comfortable being themselves, sharing their vulnerabilities, and asking for help when they need it. Selfless communities build bridges between people, connecting them on a deeper level and creating bonds that last a lifetime.

The greatest communities are those that embody selfless compassion—not just in words, but in action. They are places where people don't just think about kindness; they live it. And as each individual contributes to the collective good, the entire community benefits. The more compassion you show, the more it spreads, uplifting everyone in its path.

Ask yourself: What communities am I a part of? Do I service my communities more than I take from them?

Action step: Find one way to contribute to your community this week through selfless service. Whether it's volunteering, helping a neighbor, or simply offering a kind word to someone in need, take action to demonstrate your compassion. Reflect on how this act of giving affects both you and the people around you.

<u>Section 6:</u>

<u>Manifesting Your Dreams</u>

#51 The Call for Heart-Centered Leadership: Rising Above Fear and Division

TONE: Creative, Empowering, Imaginative, Purposeful, Motivational

How do we reform a legal system for over 300 million Americans? The riots aren't just a response to a single wrongful death; they are a symptom of the constant fear many have been living under. It's no coincidence that these riots erupted during a pandemic, a time when fear is already heightened across the world. When you pump fear into any living creature long enough, it will eventually fight back.

"Be remembered as the person who always chooses love, not fear" - CM

The constant fear that minorities experience due to their interactions with law enforcement is already overwhelming. Add to that the fear instilled by the media and government regarding COVID-19, and the uncertainty caused by the lack of leadership from elected officials, and you have a country that is deeply afraid.

"Leadership is not a position or title it is an action and example."

- Robin Sharma

The only way out of this is through strong leadership—leadership that comes from brave men and women who serve selflessly. Unfortunately, there are leaders today who are driving this country into chaos. What we need is not angry, emotional leadership, but leadership rooted in empathy, kindness, and a deep commitment to service.

True leadership is heart-centered. It is kind, empathetic, and grounded in selfless service. Sadly, this kind of leadership is not coming from our elected officials. It must come from the people. So, who will step up?

Ask Yourself: Am I, or do I know, a leader making a positive difference in my community?

Action step: Become, or support, a heart-centered leader in your community. Volunteering to help clean up after the riots is a powerful way to spark positive change.

Caution: Leadership has a dark side. Some people will lead others down destructive paths. The world is so starved for leadership that it's easy for the wrong people to rise to positions of influence. Don't blindly follow angry, self-serving leaders—they cause more harm than good.

#52 Overcoming Fear and Cynicism: Cultivating Magnificence in Life

TONE: Relentless, Courageous, Focused, Driven, Resilient

Fear, cynicism, and negativity drain the magnificence from life. Individuals can easily fall into the trap of allowing fear to control their actions and mindset. Fear, a natural instinct deeply ingrained in our behavior since the beginning of humanity, plays a crucial role in keeping us safe from danger. It helps us navigate daily challenges. However, fear can quickly evolve from a protective tool into a set of attitudes and behaviors that slowly bleed the greatness from your life.

> **"A cynical nature robs you of a happy life"**
>
> **- CM**

When someone consciously or unconsciously allows fear to dictate their thoughts and actions, they shut down their potential for personal growth and enlightenment. Cynicism is another poison to happiness and self-expansion. A cynical person doesn't just live in fear—they respond to both positive and negative situations with a knee-jerk negativity. Cynicism, like fear, stems from an instinct designed to keep us safe, but it's a symptom of an unregulated fear response.

> **"Watch what people are cynical about and you can often discover what they lack"**
>
> **- George S. Patton Jr.**

A cynic is preconditioned to see danger and negativity first. This mindset not only drains the magnificence from their own life but also impacts those around them. Cynics project their fear and negativity onto others, often leading small, constrained lives because their negative outlook prevents them from embracing new experiences and opportunities. They also repel people who are adventurous and growth-oriented, as expansion in life requires trust and a belief that the universe is fundamentally positive and supportive.

> **"What is a cynic? A man that knows the price of everything and the value of nothing"**
>
> **- Oscar Wilde**

Cultivating magnificence in your life—and in the lives of others—begins with approaching new ideas and experiences with a positive mindset. It might seem simple, but becoming a generator of goodness starts by being open-minded, trusting, and positive when faced with new experiences. This doesn't mean ignoring danger; it means beginning with a positive reaction, followed by thoughtful analysis. This approach will put you on the best path to invite magnificence into your life.

The universe will unfold before you at a rapid pace, presenting ever-expanding opportunities for greatness if you train yourself to react positively. If you want more happiness in your life, stop being cynical.

Ask yourself: In what ways am I being cynical? Am I predisposed to dislike, distrust, or react negatively to certain things?

Action step: First, identify something you're fearful of. Then, break your cycle of fear-based thinking by exploring what you've been conditioned to dislike. Look for positive traits, attributes, and features to help reduce your fear or negative response. Repeat this process until you stop draining magnificence and start cultivating it.

#53 The Champion's Mindset:
Unstoppable Persistence and the Path to Victory

TONE: Compassionate, Empowering, Loving, Authentic, Inspiring

Average people never truly decide what they want, so they wander from job to job, chasing fleeting desires until they eventually give up. For amateurs, persistence is rarely a factor because they haven't focused on any single goal long enough to truly understand what it takes to win. Without a clear vision, it's easy to get distracted by short-term challenges, leading to a cycle of giving up and starting over. The result is a life spent drifting, with no real sense of achievement or fulfillment.

> **"The difference between an amateur and professional is professionals don't know when to throw in the towel."**
>
> **- CM**

When pros decide what they want, they burn that vision into their minds daily. This isn't a casual or fleeting thought—it becomes an obsession. They focus on obtaining their goal at almost any cost, to the point where resilience becomes the defining factor of their success. Amateurs often admire this level of dedication but fail to understand that champions aren't performing for applause; they're simply following their passion with laser-like focus and refusing to look back. They reach a mental state where giving up is no longer an option. For them, failure isn't just unlikely—it's unthinkable.

The great ones know that the longer they hang tough, the greater their chances of victory. What looks like superhuman effort to the outside world is really just the manifestation of world-class mental clarity and determination. Champions don't see setbacks as defeats; they see them as stepping stones toward their ultimate goal. Each failure is just another lesson learned, another opportunity to refine their approach and come back stronger. This mindset allows them to keep pushing forward long after others would have quit.

When champions decide what they want, they focus on the details. They don't just set vague goals; they define them down to the very last detail. This level of specificity gives them a clear roadmap to follow, and they go after it with everything they've got. Their sense of purpose and their unwavering persistence is an unstoppable combination. Once they've convinced themselves that success is the only outcome, they become relentless in their pursuit.

> **"The Key of persistence opens all doors closed by resistance."**
>
> **- John Di Lemme.**

While the rest of the world watches with doubt, disbelief, or even jealousy, champions talk themselves into believing that winning is their destiny and failure is simply not an option. This unshakable belief in their ability to succeed is what fuels them through the toughest challenges, the longest hours, and the most painful moments. Winning isn't a matter of chance—it's the inevitable result of their dedication, focus, and mental strength. Champions persist not because they're fearless, but because they've conditioned their minds to see failure as impossible. This winning expectation is what sets them apart, driving them to endure pain, sacrifice, and hardship until they ultimately achieve their goals.

Ask yourself: On a scale from one to ten am I being persistent in going for my goals and dreams?

Action step: Take notice of when you stop trying. When you recognize that you are giving up decide to not stop and persist until the outcome you originally wanted is accomplished.

#54 Manifesting a New Reality:
The Power of Collective Consciousness

TONE: Confident, Action-Oriented, Courageous, Purposeful, Empowering

The population at large is becoming increasingly aware of how powerful our consciousness and minds truly are. This evolution of thought is creating a neural network of awakened minds, individuals who understand the limitless potential of human consciousness. As more people awaken to this reality, the collective intentions of loving and compassionate thoughts will be the driving force that can—and will—shift humanity to a higher level of prosperity and fulfillment.

> **"The tragedy is that we are not living the miracle all the time"**
>
> **- CM**

However, while the momentum of conscious thinking is undeniably on the rise, it is not a guaranteed outcome that humanity will automatically ascend to the next level of collective consciousness. There are still many negative forces at work—fear, hatred, greed, and ignorance—that pollute the minds of individuals and cause destruction both within ourselves and to the planet we share. This negativity often holds people back, trapping them in cycles of despair and preventing them from seeing the light of possibility.

To shift the balance and guide humanity toward a brighter future, we must share our love and spread the wisdom of compassion with those who have been conditioned to live in fear and hate. It's important to understand that helping someone open their mind to a new way of thinking requires patience, empathy, and understanding. True change doesn't come from convincing or arguing. When you try to convince someone out of a belief they didn't convince themselves into, you rarely create lasting transformation. Real change happens through inspiration and heart-centered leadership.

> **"The mind is everything. What you think you become."**
>
> **– Buddha**

Heart-centered leadership is the key to inspiring the most profound evolution of thought. Leaders who operate from a place of love and compassion, rather than fear and control, have the greatest potential to spark a collective awakening. This movement toward higher consciousness has already begun, and with each passing day, new leaders are emerging, ready to guide others toward a more awakened way of living. The intentions have been set, and with the amazing human ability to manifest our thoughts into reality, I believe we are not far from a significant shift.

The power we hold as human beings is that we can literally manifest an infinite number of possibilities with our minds. Every day, we consciously and unconsciously manifest things into our lives—sometimes without even realizing it. And when our thoughts align with love, the results can feel like miracles. The sad reality, though, is that many of us are not living in a constant state of miracle manifesting, even though it is our natural state of being to do so.

"The best way to find yourself is to lose yourself in the service of others."

– Mahatma Gandhi

Ask yourself: What can I do today to be the leader others are looking for, and how can I inspire them to live and act with love?

Action step: Spend time each day consciously focusing on positive, loving thoughts. Meditate on how you can share this energy with those around you. Lead by example, showing others how to live with love and compassion, and take one small action today that spreads positivity to someone who needs it.

#55 Defining Success:
The Key to Fulfillment and Momentum

TONE: Bold, Fearless, Empowering, Confident, Uplifting

Success with others begins with first defining success for yourself. Most people go through life without ever taking the time to explore and define what success truly means to them. In many cultures, especially in the United States, the media, our families, and societal norms have traditionally defined success as the accumulation of material possessions or how much money we have in the bank. However, the definition of success is far more complex and personal than that. True success encompasses many factors, such as good health, meaningful relationships, contribution to others, happiness, and peace of mind.

"The art of success is a skill anyone can master"
- CM

"Gratitude turns what we have into enough."
– Aesop

The problem is that society's traditional conditioning often teaches us that success only comes from hard work and struggle. We've been led to believe that without difficulty, success isn't real or valid. But this is a misconception. There are countless moments of success in our lives if we know where to look. Success doesn't always have to be hard-won or filled with sacrifice. Many of us have experienced success through synchronicity, serendipity, and effortless ease—those magical moments when things just seem to fall into place without strain.

One of the main obstacles to embracing success is the belief that it must be difficult to be meaningful. This mindset can blind us to the many small wins and moments of success that occur every day. The trick that massively successful people use to create more fulfillment in their lives is to honor the everyday moments of success, no matter how small. They recognize that by celebrating and appreciating these moments, they can generate more momentum and fulfillment.

Success is a matter of perception. The perception of how big you are winning becomes the reality of how big you are winning. When you choose to honor even the smallest victories, you create a positive cycle that builds momentum in your life. The more you celebrate your wins, the more confident, happy, and fulfilled you become. This positive energy naturally attracts more success and opportunities for growth, leading to even bigger wins in the future.

By cultivating an attitude of gratitude and choosing to recognize the success already present in your life, you open yourself up to more abundance. Success isn't just about the end goal—it's about enjoying the journey and appreciating every step along the way. When you redefine success on your own terms, you'll find that life becomes more fulfilling and that each win, no matter how small, propels you forward toward a magnificent future.

"**Success is not the key to happiness. Happiness is the key to success. If you love what you are doing, you will be successful.**"

– Albert Schweitzer

Ask yourself: In what ways am I already succeeding that I'm not fully appreciating, and how can I build on this success to create bigger wins?

Action step: Take a few moments to reflect on your current successes, big or small. Write down three ways you are winning in your life right now that you may not have fully appreciated. Next, build on these wins by identifying one new action you can take to create even more success in your future.

#56 Reclaiming Focus:
Aligning with Your Divine Purpose

TONE: Celebratory, Joyful, Energizing, Fun, Uplifting

In a world of constant distraction, we are increasingly being programmed by the agendas and influences of others. The bombardment of media, social expectations, and outside opinions pulls us in countless directions. We lose sight of our passion and purpose because we are constantly responding to external forces that shape our culture and society. While some of these influences may have positive intentions, most of them merely interrupt and divert us from our true purpose. They distance us from the connection to our divine source, the very essence of our being.

"Our connection to the divine ultimate intelligence can manifest magnificent results into our lives as long as we know how to ask the right questions" - CM

To regain control of our lives, we must look inward and reconnect with that divine source within us. It's essential to remember that we have unlimited power to direct the outcome of our own lives. This power lies in our ability to manifest our thoughts into reality. The art of manifestation isn't just a mystical idea—it's a practice, and like any practice, it becomes easier and more effective with conscious, consistent effort. When you align your thoughts and intentions with your heart's greatest vision for the future, you tap into an unlimited source of creative power.

Aligning with your heart-centered vision for your future will transform your reality into what you truly desire. But this journey begins with trusting in the divine—trusting that there is a greater intelligence guiding you and supporting your aspirations. Many people lose their way because they place more faith in the influences of the world than in themselves. To break free from this external programming, you must believe deeply in your own ability to create and manifest the life you want.

"The future belongs to those who can conceive it, believe it, and achieve it."

– Unknown

Once you have a clear vision of your magnificent future, commit to it wholeheartedly. Make it your definite purpose. When you align your purpose with the divine, the universe will begin to conspire with you to manifest that reality. The path will unfold, and you will find that doors open where you once saw walls. Your heart-centered vision becomes a magnet for opportunities, people, and resources that will help you bring your dreams to life.

The future belongs to those who can envision, believe, and achieve their goals. The key is to stay focused despite the distractions that surround you. Trust yourself, trust the divine, and have the courage to follow your heart. With every step you take toward your vision, you'll grow stronger and more capable of manifesting the reality you desire.

> **Ask yourself:** Am I on the path to my most magnificent future, or am I being distracted by external influences?

> **Action step**: Set aside time today to reflect on your heart-centered vision for your future. Write it down in as much detail as possible—what does it look like? How do you feel living this reality? Then, identify one small action you can take today to begin aligning your life with that vision.

#57 The Power of Synchronicity: Embracing Divine Appointments and Leadership

TONE: Open-Minded, Bold, Courageous, Growth-Oriented, Uplifting

Some believe that when synchronicities happen in life—such as meeting the perfect person at the perfect time to solve an impossible problem—it is a miracle. While these moments certainly feel miraculous, I believe the miracle is happening all the time, and the real tragedy is that we're not fully experiencing these divine appointments on a regular basis. The universe is always aligning an infinite number of time and space events to manifest any result we can imagine. As free-thinking humans, it is in our divine nature to use conscious thought to create our desires with effortless ease.

> **"The miracle is happening all the time, and the real tragedy is that we're not fully recognizing the divine appointments as the way of life" - CM**

The biggest challenge we face as a species is the misuse of our miraculous power to manifest. Instead of using our thoughts to create love, abundance, and connection, many of us are trapped in fear-based thinking. The lack of heart-centered leadership on this planet has distorted our loving, compassionate nature and morphed it into ego-driven fear. This fear separates us from our true potential and blinds us to the miracles that could be unfolding in every moment.

The good news is that we have the power to ascend to a higher level of consciousness and experience a never-ending series of miracles. By simply remembering our divine nature and walking with full faith in love, we can reclaim our ability to manifest positive, life-changing synchronicities. We live in a friendly universe, and the bold actions of heart-centered leaders will guide us back to this realization. Love, compassion, and support are our natural states, and by embracing them, we can restore the world to a place of abundance, prosperity, and harmony.

It's time for us to step into heart-centered leadership and inspire others to do the same. Leadership doesn't always come from those with titles or positions of power. True leadership comes from individuals who act from a place of love, integrity, and courage. When we lead from the heart, we naturally attract synchronicities that help us fulfill our purpose and assist others along their journey. By inspiring others, we can cure the deficit of leadership we currently see on this planet and restore abundance for all.

Be brave, be bold, and trust in your intuition. You instinctively know how to be a beacon of love and light for others. Overflow with love, and watch as the universe conspires to bring people, opportunities, and miracles into your life. The power to change the world lies within each of us, and it begins by embracing our role as heart-centered leaders.

> **"The universe is not outside of you. Look inside yourself; everything that you want, you already are."**
>
> **– Rumi**

"When you truly trust yourself, you attract the right people, places, and opportunities to fulfill your purpose." – Unknown

Ask yourself: How can I be a heart-centered leader today, and what actions can I take to inspire others to do the same?

Action step: Reflect on a recent synchronicity in your life and how it felt. Take a bold step today by following your intuition to help or inspire someone else. Act as a heart-centered leader and watch how the universe aligns to support your actions.

#58 The Power of Discipline: Crafting a Life of Purpose and Legacy

TONE: Driven, Purposeful, Passionate, Focused, Empowering

The quality of your life is directly proportional to the amount of discipline you are willing to cultivate. True peace of mind and long-lasting fulfillment come from being 100% honest with yourself about your efforts. Anxiety, stress, and worry often arise not from external circumstances but from the inner conflict of knowing you aren't giving your best. When you fall short of your true potential, the mind becomes restless, and dissatisfaction seeps in. Discipline is the bridge between where you are now and the lifestyle of your dreams.

> **"You either pay the price in discipline or you pay the price with regret, either way there is no free ride."**
>
> **- CM**

In today's world, distractions are abundant. Excessive worldly pleasures, procrastination, and fleeting comforts may seem harmless in the moment, but over time, they can erode the foundation of the magnificent life you are capable of creating. These distractions don't just keep you from achieving your short-term goals—they also prevent you from building a lasting legacy. While discipline and sacrifice aren't always glamorous or popular topics, they are the keys to unlocking true fulfillment and a life of purpose.

Discipline is about making consistent choices—the small, often difficult decisions that compound over time to create lasting success. It's the simple actions that are easy to do, but just as easy not to do. The difference between a person who is satisfied, happy, and thriving and someone who is nervous, fearful, and disempowered is often rooted in discipline. Those who thrive have made sacrifices consistently enough to turn discipline into a habit, while those who struggle often haven't committed to the necessary sacrifices.

> **"Discipline is choosing between what you want now and what you want most."**
>
> **– Unknown**

Sacrifice isn't about deprivation. It's about making the conscious choice to give up short-term pleasure for long-term gain. It's the discipline of choosing what you want most over what you want now. When you master this mindset, you'll find that discipline becomes less about restriction and more about empowerment. Each disciplined action builds momentum and creates a ripple effect in every area of your life.

When you make sacrifice and discipline a way of life, the rewards are far greater than the temporary discomfort of giving something up. Peace of mind, confidence, and a sense of purpose naturally follow. The more you align your actions with your highest goals, the more resilient and focused you become. Discipline also allows you to eliminate distractions, making it easier to take consistent, empowered actions.

In essence, discipline is freedom—the freedom to live a life of intention, the freedom to achieve your dreams, and the freedom to create a legacy that matters. The more disciplined you are, the more control you have over your destiny.

"We must all suffer one of two things: the pain of discipline or the pain of regret."

– Jim Rohn

Ask yourself: What can I sacrifice in my life today to eliminate distractions and make disciplined actions easier to accomplish?

Action step: Reflect on one area of your life where you know you've been distracted or inconsistent. Identify a specific sacrifice you can make today that will eliminate those distractions and make disciplined actions easier to maintain. Commit to this sacrifice for the next week and observe how it transforms your focus and productivity.

#59 The Power of the Future: Fueling Your Passion and Purpose

TONE: Generous, Compassionate, Warm, Loving, Uplifting

The power of the future has the potential to ignite your heart with a burning, lightning-hot passion. This passion, when manifested on a foundation of purpose, has the strength to propel you through any challenge life throws your way. The key to this unstoppable force lies in the relationship you build with your own future. The strongest foundation for your passion will be rooted in your connection with your future self—a version of you that embodies your fullest potential, your deepest desires, and your most magnificent achievements.

> "The quality of the questions we ask ourselves will be in direct proportion to the quality of our lives." – CM

When you establish a relationship with your future self, your emotional state in the present becomes one of happiness and confidence. Knowing that your future self is not only possible but inevitable, you start attracting that reality into your present. Every decision, every action, and every thought aligns with the vision of who you are becoming. Your future self becomes your best friend, guiding you toward the lifestyle of your dreams.

To discover your purpose and passion, look no further than your future self. Simply ask, "What does my most magnificent future self-do, and what brings them the deepest fulfillment?" By envisioning the version of yourself that is living a life of purpose, success, and joy, you begin to unravel the mysteries of your own desires. The questions you ask yourself hold immense power—questions shape your thoughts, direct your energy, and ultimately, determine the quality of your life.

> "Your future self is the compass guiding you through the present—listen closely, and you'll never lose your way."
>
> – Unknown

The quality of your life is in direct proportion to the quality of the questions you ask. When you ask profound, purpose-driven questions, you set in motion a process that leads you to clarity, vision, and action. Your mind, conscious and subconscious, begins searching for answers, solutions, and opportunities that align with your desired future. As a result, you gain clarity about what truly drives you and what steps you need to take to turn your dreams into reality.

Don't settle for less when you have the power to create the lifestyle of your dreams. The more you connect with your future self—the one who has already achieved what you aspire to—the more you can feel the certainty that success is inevitable. Passion and purpose will guide your every move when you know exactly what you're working toward. By cultivating a relationship with your future self, you step into your present with purpose, knowing that the best is yet to come.

> "Your future is created by what you do today, not tomorrow."
>
> – Robert Kiyosaki

Ask yourself: What does my most magnificent future self do, and how can I start embodying those qualities today?

Action step: Set aside time today to visualize your most magnificent future self. Write down their qualities, habits, and what makes them deeply fulfilled. Reflect on what steps you can take now to align your present self with the person you want to become.

#60 Manifesting Magic:
Turning Thoughts into Things through Passion and Purpose

TONE: Creative, Visionary, Empowering, Purposeful, Motivational

There is a powerful truth about human potential: we can manifest our thoughts into reality. The ability to turn an idea into something tangible, to bring a dream into existence, is one of the most extraordinary powers we possess. However, manifesting this magic doesn't happen by accident. It requires intention, focus, passion, and purpose. When your thoughts are aligned with your deepest passions and fueled by a sense of purpose, you unlock the magic to create the life you desire.

"Your ability to manifest your thoughts into things is directed related to your rate of vibrations and how intense your daily routine is" - CM

At the core of manifestation is the belief that our thoughts are powerful. Every great invention, piece of art, and personal achievement started as a thought, an idea in someone's mind. Thoughts are the seeds of creation, but without the right energy and action behind them, they remain just that—seeds. Passion is the fuel that transforms those seeds into reality. Passion gives life to your thoughts, empowering you to take bold actions and stay committed to your vision, even when challenges arise.

"Whatever the mind of man can conceive and believe, it can achieve."

– Napoleon Hill

To manifest anything meaningful, your thoughts must be aligned with a strong sense of purpose. Purpose gives your passion direction. It's the driving force that guides you when things get tough and ensures that the things you manifest are in alignment with your core values and your highest goals. When your purpose is clear, your thoughts become more focused, and your actions become more intentional. You're not just chasing dreams for the sake of it—you're creating a life that reflects who you truly are and what you're meant to contribute to the world.

Passion without purpose can lead to burnout. You may find yourself pursuing things that don't truly fulfill you, leaving you feeling exhausted and unmotivated. Similarly, purpose without passion can leave you feeling stagnant, knowing what you should do but lacking the energy and excitement to take action. It's only when passion and purpose come together that the magic of manifestation happens. This powerful combination creates momentum, driving you to turn your thoughts into tangible results.

Manifestation is not wishful thinking—it's a process that requires clarity, intention, and persistent action. To manifest magic in your life, start by getting clear on what you want. What is the vision you have for yourself? What dreams light a fire in your heart? Once you know what you want, you must then align your thoughts and energy with that vision. This means not only thinking about your goals but also believing in your ability to achieve them. Doubt and fear can block your ability to manifest, so it's important to build a mindset of faith and confidence.

Visualization is a powerful tool in the process of manifestation. When you visualize your future with passion, you create a mental image of the life you desire. This image serves as a roadmap, helping you stay focused on your goals and giving you the motivation to take action. But visualization alone isn't enough—you must back it up with purpose-driven action. Purpose is what turns your vision into a plan, and passion is what drives you to execute that plan with enthusiasm and persistence.

Another key to manifesting magic is understanding the law of attraction. The energy you put out into the world—through your thoughts, emotions, and actions—attracts similar energy back to you. When you focus on your passion and purpose with a positive, empowered mindset, you naturally attract opportunities, people, and resources that align with your vision. This is where the magic happens: when your energy is aligned with your goals, the universe begins to conspire in your favor.

However, it's important to remember that manifesting magic requires patience and persistence. Big dreams take time. The path to manifesting your desires may be filled with obstacles, but these challenges are part of the process. They help you grow, refine your vision, and develop the resilience needed to reach your goals. Don't give up when things get tough—keep your passion alive, stay connected to your purpose, and trust that the magic will unfold in its own time.

The most successful people in the world are not those who never face challenges but those who continue to move forward despite them. They understand that manifestation is a journey. Every action they take, no matter how small, brings them one step closer to turning their thoughts into things. When you stay committed to your vision with passion and purpose, the universe responds to your efforts, and the impossible starts to become possible.

Ask yourself: Do I really know what my passion and purpose is?

Action step: Take a moment to reflect on your most passionate goals. Write down one specific goal that aligns with your deepest sense of purpose. Create a simple plan of action and take the first step today, no matter how small. Visualize yourself achieving that goal and focus on how it feels. Let this visualization fuel your actions moving forward.